Conducting Support Groups for Elementary Children K-6

A Guide for Educators and Other Professionals

by

Jerry Moe and Peter Ways

JOHNSON INSTITUTE®

Minneapolis

From the library of:
Stan Brein, M.S., N.C.S.P.
Licensed Specialist in School Psychology
Denton, Texas

To our children,

Josh, Aubrey, Megan;
Heather, Carol, Martha, Peter,
who, in the ways they light their
own journeys,
help us to be more loving
on our own.

Copyright ©1991 by the Johnson Institute. All rights reserved. No part of this book may be reproduced or transmitted in any form or by any means, electronic or mechanical, including photocopying, recording, or by any information storage and retrieval system without express permission in writing from the publisher, Johnson Institute, 7151 Metro Blvd., Suite 250, Minneapolis, Minnesota 55439-2122.

Library of Congress Cataloging-in-Publication Data

Moe, Jerry.

    Conducting support groups for elementary children K-6: a guide for educators and other professionals / Jerry Moe and Peter Ways.
      p.   cm.
    Includes bibliographical references (p.).
    ISBN (invalid) 1-56246-018-1
    1. Group guidance in education. 2. Peer-group counseling of students.   I. Ways, Peter 1928-   II. Title.
LB1027.5.M558   1991
372.14 ' 044—dc20   91-3820
                                     CIP

Contents

Acknowledgments

This book would never have happened without the love and support of many family members, colleagues, and friends. Our special thanks go to the staff of Sequoia Hospital Alcohol and Drug Recovery Center. Under the catalytic leadership of Dr. Barry Rosen, Lynda Voorhees, and Dori Dysland, the staff has dedicated itself to assisting all family members, especially children, in the recovery process. To those individuals who have pioneered this work, especially the board and advisory board members of the National Association for Children of Alcoholics—their courage, strength, and conviction have guided us. Martin Fleming's excellent book, *Conducting Support Groups for Students Affected by Chemical Dependence,* served as a guide and a source of inspiration. Thank you, Martin!

In addition to their support and enthusiasm for the book, Nancy Coxwell, Gretchen Gundrum, and Michelle Moe reviewed earlier drafts and made many useful suggestions. Virginia Jenny offered valuable feedback as she computerized the text.

To our editor, Lenore Franzen of the Johnson Institute, our sincere gratitude. Her warmth, love, single-mindedness, and enthusiasm have continuously encouraged us and deeply enriched this project.

Lastly, and most importantly, our love and gratitude to all those youngsters we've had the privilege to serve in support groups—thank you for being our teachers.

Introduction

1

"There is only one subject-matter for education, and that is Life in all its manifestations."

—Alfred North Whitehead

For the past several decades, our core classes and programs have emphasized teaching facts and concepts—*cognitive* learning—and largely ignored affective growth and development. What does this imbalance mean for our students? We believe that they learn less successfully and that we and our society will feel the effects now and for a long time to come.

We have written this book with the conviction that school-based support groups can help correct this imbalance and make a lasting difference in the lives of our children. In support groups, children become aware of their feelings, learn to express their emotions, grow in self-esteem, and develop interactive skills and stable value systems that come from within.

Support groups for elementary school children grades K-6 are an essential educational strategy that engages students in the *affective* side of learning and "Life." And support groups provide a way for many hurting children to get help. Nick is one youngster who did.

> Nick was an angry second-grader. He lived with his mom, an active alcoholic, whose behavior was erratic and unpredictable. Nick's dad had left the scene years before. Many times Nick was left alone at night to care for his younger brother because their mother was out drinking. In school, Nick sometimes intimidated the smaller children and had angry outbursts that were triggered by the slightest provocation. About halfway through the school year, Nick's teacher, at her wits end, referred Nick to the school's child study team for assessment and evaluation.

There are many Nicks in our elementary schools. They are children whose ability to learn and mature emotionally is seriously impaired, for they find themselves forced to channel all their energies into coping with the problems and powerfully conflicting feelings that have been created by a loved one's addiction to alcohol or other drugs.

This is not to say that all the problems in the classroom are caused by chemical dependence. Many children face imposing living problems and issues regarding emotional health without chemical dependence in their homes. They reside with a chronically ill parent, or a workaholic, or in a one-parent home. They live with abandonment, betrayal, invalidation, or abuse. Yet, the use and abuse of alcohol and other drugs remains the number one health problem in our society. And children from homes with chemical dependence are too often victims of abandonment, betrayal, invalidation, and abuse. Children in homes like these—children like Nick—need help from outside the home. School-based support groups can provide that help.

The school study team placed Nick in a special education class, but his acting out worsened. Finally, near the end of the school year, Nick was sent to his first support group. The group facilitator described Nick as "generally quiet but acts out occasionally. He seems to like group but doesn't participate much." During the following school year, Nick took part in a second support group. One of the group activities was drawing. Through his drawings, Nick started to gain confidence and slowly began to speak up. In his drawings, Nick showed pictures of bottles, of "Dad not there," and of his mother drunk.

Nick was lucky. He had a teacher who recognized that there was something amiss, something that was keeping him from learning effectively. Fortunately, there are many teachers like Nick's. These teachers have made time in their classrooms to allow their students to air their feelings and to help their students grow in self-esteem. Thankfully, some school systems have recognized that their responsibility definitely extends into the realm of affective learning and have instituted such practices system-wide. Yet too many Nicks remain.

This book is written for teachers, educational administrators, and other professionals concerned about all children who are affected by chemical dependence and living problems that impair their ability to learn. It will help you discover how support groups can make a major and essential contribution to prevent substance abuse, to modify tensions and behaviors related to other personal and living problems, and to sustain and enhance children's emotional growth, energy, and vitality.

It took time, but as Nick continued to attend both special education classes and the support group, his behavior improved. By the middle of fourth grade, Nick was back in "regular" class for part of each day. In fifth grade, he was elected class president.

Nick still struggles at times. Wanting to fix his mom and her alcoholism, he goes through periods when he minimizes and denies her problem. But Nick's journey is a relatively peaceful one now. He is making progress in school and is steadily attaining useful social skills.

Why Involve the Schools?

If parents really are children's primary educators, core community, and most effective communicators and enforcers of values and rules, why involve the schools in this "family business"? Experienced teachers, school administrators, and counselors know why. The school is a close partner to parents. Home and school are two of the four most powerful influences—along with peers and television—on the emotional, social, and intellectual development of our children. If teachers and schools act as allies with parents (or guardians), they can do much to enhance that development. Support groups can be a very influential tool in helping parents and teachers bring this about. Evidence Janie's story:

> After attending a presentation on student support groups offered by the PTA, Janie's mother decided to refer her fourth-grade daughter to one of the school's groups. Quiet and shy, Janie said very little during the eight-week program. She was one of those children who too easily fall through the cracks: average grades, kept to herself, never a discipline problem. In mid-year, Janie's fourth-grade teacher referred her to another group. The facilitator noticed that Janie was increasingly withdrawn, responded to questions very flatly, and often visited the school nurse with complaints of headaches, stomach pains, and minor injuries. Toward the end of the cycle of group meetings, the facilitator asked to speak to Janie alone. After only a few words with

the facilitator, Janie's eyes filled with tears. She grabbed the facilitator's hand and cried, "My dad drinks too much beer!"

Because of the school's willingness to offer support groups and her mother's willingness to work with them, Janie was at last able to get her problem out in the open. Now, it could be dealt with. Janie's experience points to a number of additional reasons why basing support group programs in the schools makes so much sense:

- Children's support groups need to be where children are, and children are in school a lot of the time.

- In school, children spend their time not only with peers, but also with people specifically trained to work with children: teachers, school counselors, and administrators. These people provide a natural pool of support group facilitators.

- Like Janie, many other elementary school children are at high risk of suffering the effects of chemical dependence or of becoming chemically dependent themselves.

- Without the schools' participation in helping such children, they probably will not be helped at all.

  With her mom's hesitant approval, Janie next took part in an educational support group with other children whose homes were also darkened and confused by chemical dependence. The following year, Janie began to blossom. Continuing in the program, she found her group to be a safe place to reveal her feelings to others who understood. Something clicked for Janie, and she truly accepted that her dad's drinking was not her fault. As her confidence grew, Janie began to take care of herself and refused to be devastated by her dad's drinking.

Support groups can work in a variety of other settings as well:

- churches
- recreational programs

5

- scouting programs
- juvenile correctional programs and facilities
- community agencies

Regardless of the particular setting, the success of a support group depends on two factors. The first is the group's relevance to the children's needs. The effective support group program constantly strives to "fit" the requirements of its members and speak clearly to the children's needs through continual adaptation, refinement, and modification. The second factor is group facilitators the children can readily identify with and trust—individuals who know the cultural and social nuances of the children and can speak their language.

Support Groups as a Prevention Strategy

While many people agree that schools need to pay more attention to preventing alcohol and other drug use and abuse, they also argue that cognitive learning—giving students more facts and concepts—is the answer. But knowledge alone won't "cure" chemical dependence. Why? Because, like diabetes or smallpox, chemical dependence is a disease, not simply a matter of willpower or lack of self-control. So knowledge alone doesn't constitute an effective prevention strategy.

Good teachers know this. They have witnessed the curiosity and sadness on the faces of children who have viewed a slide show or video on chemical dependence. They have heard children crying for unspoken reasons. They have listened to children asking to stay after school because they were afraid to go home. Good teachers know that presenting facts and concepts goes far in raising questions and feelings and in elevating unconscious and unanswered needs to the level of awareness. But good teachers also know that presenting facts and concepts doesn't go far enough.

No one—especially a child—learns to feel by listening to a lecture on feelings. A person learns to feel only within a trusting atmosphere where he or she can safely risk expressing feelings. To learn about their feelings and to learn how to make healthy choices in relation to their feelings, children need the *experience* of communicating feelings to and with others. The same can be said about values clarification, emotional healing, and developing compassion: *Experience is the best teacher.*

Our experience has taught us that the best setting for children to explore their feelings is in small peer support groups. Moreover, our experience has also taught us the following about support groups:

- Values are more likely to be strengthened and clarified in small support groups.
- Children with problems find camaraderie and constructive peer support in small groups.
- Children enjoy learning from one another and can encourage one another to take risks.
- Support groups provide a safe and confidential place for children to express their feelings.
- The group format is excellent for learning life skills.
- In small groups, children learn that it's okay to ask for help and that they are not alone.
- Children who have been wounded in the family can find healing among loving, trusting peers.

Given the limited resources of many schools, the teaching loads and time restrictions of teachers, and the number of children to be served, support groups appear to be the most educationally sound and realistic means of meeting the many needs outlined above. The camaraderie and process of groups can involve many children who, because of their age and development, would not respond to individual support and counseling, even if it were possible to make them available.

Why the Focus on Chemical Dependence?

If support groups can help with the life problems that cover a spectrum broader than that encompassed by chemical dependence, why focus on chemical dependence? We do so for two main reasons.

First of all, chemical dependence is the United States' foremost health problem. It is the leading cause of productive years of life lost (that is, years during which a person functions poorly or not at all because of alcohol or other drugs). For example, if an eight-year-old, who is riding in a car with a parent who is drunk or high, dies as a result of an accident, sixty-seven productive years of life are lost. Chemical dependence is also the leading cause of lost time from or at work.

The second reason support groups focus on chemical dependence is because we have had the most experience with the children of chemically dependent families. Over and over, we have seen support groups provide visible and tangible aid and a more hopeful view of life for many children of chemically dependent families.

We know that children get caught in a cycle when troubles exist within a family. The cycle goes like this:

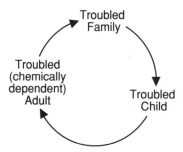

Troubled Family

Troubled Child

Troubled (chemically dependent) Adult

We also know that the cycle is clearest in families with chemical dependence. Those who work in the field of chemical dependence know well that the earlier we can break this cycle, the greater and more lasting will be the benefits for the child and the family.

What Kind of Support Groups Are Needed?

Since the success of support groups depends, first of all, on their meeting the needs of children, and since the needs of the many children in an elementary school are varied, the question naturally arises, "Just what sort of support groups are needed?" We suggest two:

- *Concerned Persons* groups
- *Living Skills* groups

Concerned Persons groups speak to the needs of children who are members of a family in which chemical dependence is a reality. These groups provide children a welcome, caring, and helping environment where they can safely deal with the many problems living with a chemically dependent person entails. *Living Skills* groups involve children in a process that helps them make better decisions about their lives, provides them with a clearer view of who they truly are, and helps them improve their self-esteem and self-worth. As you can readily imagine, the techniques and skills involved in these two types of groups will overlap and complement each other.

What's the Bottom Line?

This book will do much to help you establish support groups and support group programs for elementary school children. However, you should be aware that this book is one of many resources available to you. They include training workshops, seminars, films and videos, prevention curricula, and other books. A list of these resources is provided for you in the Appendices of this book.

By providing and conducting support groups for our children, we are convinced that elementary schools will make a difference in preventing our society's number one health problem, chemical dependence. At the same time, schools will also contribute significantly to the broader and more fundamental goal of promoting all children's healthy psychosocial development. By means of small group techniques, the teachers, counselors, and administrators of our K-6 schools can be a major factor in breaking the cycle that affects so many children in our schools and society, especially children like Janie.

> After her participation in the school's support group program, Janie, along with her mom, was referred by the facilitator to a community agency that provid-

ed groups for children of chemically dependent families. Janie has been participating in that program and continues to emerge from her shell, slowly making more friends and talking about her feelings with safe people. Even though her dad still drinks, Janie is coping in a healthier way and is now able to truly play and smile. She has fewer headaches and stomach pains. Her group leader sees Janie as more confident, as feeling better about herself, and notes that she is able to speak about her feelings more readily.

Recently Janie volunteered to be on a panel of children who spoke to the school about alcohol and other drugs during Red Ribbon Week. In tears, Janie shared how her absent dad was an alcoholic and how much she missed him. "But," she added, "I know now that I didn't make my dad sick and that I can't make him better. But I can take better care of myself."

Within the framework of a community-wide prevention effort, schools can play a pivotal role both in promoting health in general and in preventing alcohol and other drug problems in particular. By providing and conducting support groups for elementary children, schools can give these children the encouragement and support they need to grow into adults who possess strong and internalized identities and values, whose self-esteem is enduring, and whose lives manifest continued joy and growth. There is no clearer, or better, bottom line.

The Challenges We Face 2

We live in a culture preoccupied with "youth", with staying young in mind and appearance. Hundreds of products purport to preserve or enhance our youthfulness. "Staying young" is promoted as a major societal value. Paradoxically, however, our core social values and priorities are not geared toward children, and our commitment to quality care for children is slipping badly.

- From 1978 to 1987 government spending on the elderly rose 52%; spending on children decreased 4%.

- The United States has one of the highest infant mortality rates among the world's industrialized countries.

- The United States ranks 19th, behind Libya and Cuba (among other developed nations), in teacher/pupil ratio.

- Each year, 250,000 seriously underweight babies are born in the United States, but nutritional programs for women, infants, and children are decreasing.

- One-fourth of all children under the age of six live in families that exist below the poverty level (annual income of $12,500). The United States has one of the highest child poverty rates of any industrialized nation.

- Support for child care in the United States is far below that of some other industrialized nations and far below the need.

Challenges to Children

Given the above manifestations of our national priorities, it's not surprising that the Senate Select Committee on Children, Youth, and Families found that the children of the United States are at greater risk for major physical and mental health problems than children in most of the world's other developed countries.

Put simply, it's not easy growing up today.

- Every 47 seconds a child is abused or neglected.
- Every 4 1/2 minutes a child runs away from home.
- Every 36 minutes a child is injured or killed by a gun.
- In 1989, there were 2.4 million *reported* cases of child abuse (a 10% increase over 1988).
- Among fourth-graders, 36% feel "pressure" to use alcohol.

It's tough being a kid today.

Children must "grow up" too fast. They are making major life choices about things like sex and alcohol and other drugs that they are not yet ready to make. Many youngsters aren't given adequate time, attention, and support to be just children, or to develop their own identities. When this happens, children grow up emotionally blocked or underdeveloped, with unhealed childhood wounds and little clarity about their values. Furthermore, societal and familial pressures impede the classroom learning process; children come to school ill-prepared and ill-equipped to learn.

Emphatically, our youngest people need our thoughtful, positive help. They need it now. And they need a lot of it.

Challenges of Chemical Dependence

Alcohol and other drugs pose a major problem to our children today. They grow up in a world where their parents, peers, heroes, and heroines are commonly seen or portrayed using alcohol or other drugs, often in harmful ways. Let's look more closely at the problems U.S. children face in relation to alcohol and other drugs.

1. Alcohol and other drug use by parents, siblings, and peer groups makes a powerful impact on children. "Just Say No" and other messages to the contrary, youngsters find themselves openly influenced to experiment with alcohol and other drugs. Children do as we do, not as we say.

2. In advertising and the media, alcohol and other drugs are an integral part of many portrayals and are often glamorized or the subject of humor. Too many athletes and rock musicians—famous, materially successful, contemporary heroes and heroines to many children—openly use alcohol and other drugs.

3. Alcohol is the drug of choice for our youth. In addition to being a damaging killer on its own, alcohol is a "gateway substance"—along with tobacco—to the use of powerful, illegal ("street") drugs.

4. Chemical dependence may affect children profoundly, even *before* they themselves become involved with chemicals, or even if they themselves *never* become involved with chemicals. The greatest risk factor for a person becoming chemically dependent is growing up in a home where one or both parents, a sibling, or a grandparent is chemically dependent. For example, there are unspoken rules in the alcoholic home that strongly influence behavior patterns in children: "We must all work together to preserve the family secret (that there is an alcoholic in the family)," "None of our troubles has anything to do with alcohol," "Don't talk. Don't trust. Don't feel." Often children of alcoholics turn to compulsive behaviors to defend against their pain: self-isolation, excessive and inappropriate joking, people pleasing, striving to be perfect, acting out, smoking, and using alcohol or other drugs. Too often, these children are deeply lacking in self-esteem and self-worth.

Such are the principal challenges that substance abuse presents our children. It is crucial that we help our youngsters successfully meet and overcome these challenges, or they will continue to be hindered for the rest of their lives. Lacking such success, our children will have to face the long-term dangers—the "downstream" effects—of alcohol and other drugs. For example:

- Every 8 seconds a youngster drops out of school.

- Every 67 seconds a teenager gives birth.

- Every 7 minutes a minor is arrested for a drug-related offense; increasingly, these arrests involve younger and younger people.

- More than 75% of all young people's deaths are caused by accidents, suicide, homicide, or other forms of violence.

- 135,000 children in our society carry guns to school.

- In 1987, there were 100,000 alcohol-related U.S. deaths, equivalent to *2.7 million* years of productive life lost.

- Alcohol and other drugs are also the leading, non-fatal cause of productive years of life lost.

The American Medical Association recently stated: "Never before has one generation of American teenagers been less healthy, less cared-for, and less prepared for life than their parents were at the same age." It bears repeating: *It's tough being a kid today.*

Challenges to Parents

Parents today face an array of challenges that run parallel to those of their children. Many of today's parents never had the chance to mature emotionally at a natural pace. The *process of becoming adult* was warped for them by the speed and demands of our society and by the patterns of parents, teachers, and employers who were not themselves accorded an opportunity to heal their childhood wounds, or to acquire interactive skills and a full repertoire of feelings. It is hard to be a parent when your own upbringing did not prepare you emotionally for the task, provide the security you needed, or give you the skills (like limit setting) that one needs for being a successful parent.

Being a parent has never been an easy job. In these days of single parent households, blended families, day care, and latch-key children, it is even more difficult. Compound that by asking how one successfully raises a child in a society where TV, cinema, and the media trivialize violence by treating it more like entertainment than serious crime, where racial tensions are high, where alcohol and other drugs are ubiquitous, and where unlawful gangs influence values and behavior.

Like their own kids, many parents are faced with choices and decisions too early in life, and for which they are not prepared. Virtually everybody's kids have problems of some kind or another, many of them very significant. This creates the generation gap. Our own experiences are no longer valid contexts for evaluating a child's behavior. Few of us who are parents today were faced with the environment, the peer social structure, and the chemicals that influence today's youth.

To make matters worse, we are not trained in parenting. Society itself does not perceive a need for that. There are no standards or licensing required to carry out the most demanding and important job there is. Most of us stumble along, patterning ourselves after our own parents, who themselves had no explicit guidance or training. Parents do their best, yet sometimes lack the skills, tools, time, and energy. *It's tough being a parent today.*

Challenges to Teachers

Due to a lack of optimal support, increasing class size, shrinking school budgets, and the problems and behavior patterns many children bring to school, teachers are often hampered from doing what they do best—teach.

Instead, teachers find themselves dealing with children from complex family structures, children who may possess one or more of the major problems discussed previously. Teachers also face perplexing and persistent disciplinary problems and children whose sojourn in the class is brief, due to the mobility of today's average family. In many cases, children no longer possess the extended family ties of community and neighborhood, which once were a vital source of stability and security. Many children in today's classrooms feel forced (primarily by peers and culture) to make difficult decisions that they are unprepared to make wisely. And teachers, even the best of teachers, often feel that their hands are tied or that they are unprepared for the stresses and challenges of full-time teaching. *It's tough being a teacher today.*

Meeting the Challenges

So it's tough being a kid, tough being a parent, and tough being a teacher. Confronted with these challenges, children, parents, and teachers—instead of pulling together—too often pull apart. Most of the time, in this three-way tug-of-war, it is the children who get the worst of it.

Support group programs offer schools and their communities a way of helping children, parents, and teachers pull together. Support group programs can help meet the challenges faced by all three of these groups, break the cycle of unhealthy childhood patterns, defuse anger, reconcile emotional confusion, allow free expression of feelings, teach important life skills, and resolve serious impediments to the sort of classroom learning that teachers are so eager to provide.

By offering support groups for elementary children (K-6) and by conducting them with sensitivity, expertise, clear goals, effective pedagogy, and engaging tools, schools can play a revitalizing role in meeting the many challenges we face. Support groups let children be children, help parents do their job, and allow teachers to teach. Support groups can strengthen us—all of us—to pull together to meet the challenges posed by alcohol and other drugs and to prevail.

Overview of Support Groups

3

Many elementary schools offer prevention programs on alcohol and other drugs as part of their curriculum. These programs primarily feature instruction on alcohol, other drugs, and addiction, which is presented in an age-appropriate and non-threatening manner. Such in-class prevention programs can provide youngsters with valuable information and insight and are an important first step in building a comprehensive prevention program.

Some children, however, need a more in-depth, experiential learning format to secure the kind of support they need. This may be especially true for children of chemically dependent parents, since these children are at such a high risk themselves for developing chemical dependence, as well as other health and behavioral problems. Likewise, children from other high-stress families—families where divorce, abuse, neglect, workaholism, illness, or other difficulties are prevalent—may also need more backing than the average classroom prevention curriculum can provide. Support groups are the logical next step in assisting these children.

In addition to redressing the imbalance between cognitive and affective learning found in most elementary education (refer to Chapter 1), support groups focus on two other major goals:

- to foster education and awareness about chemicals and chemical dependence
- to provide aid, support, and a place to process feelings in difficult times

In this chapter, we will explore the goals of support groups, the types of support groups, and the elements of group design that enable support groups to keep their focus and reach their goals.

Goal #1: Fostering Education and Awareness

Children often lack basic information about alcohol, other drugs, and chemical dependence. Moreover, many children simply have not acquired sufficient healthy living skills. These deficits often make it difficult for children to learn and do their best in school. In support groups, children, like Becky in the example below, gain new insight and awareness from the information presented by the group facilitator and by listening to and observing others in the group.

> Becky was a shy, withdrawn third-grader who continually wore a scowl the first few weeks of school and who wouldn't interact much with others. But, during a support group session, Becky heard that children are not the cause of their parents' divorce. Later, what Becky had heard from the facilitator was confirmed by a couple of other children in the group who acknowledged that they used to worry they had caused their parents to split up. Buoyed by this information and support, Becky was able to share her feelings about her parents' divorce. Becky now actively plays and interacts with the other children in her class.

A little information and awareness can often make a big difference in a child's life.

Goal #2: Providing Support

Sometimes education and awareness aren't enough. For example, most children have been taught to use seat belts when riding in a car, and they are aware of what could happen to them if they were to get into an accident without being buckled up. Even so, many children use seat belts only when prodded and supported by concerned parents. Knowing what's what and acting according to what's what is not the same thing. Sometimes children need more than information.

Let's face it, most children need support, especially when the information they hear stirs up deep feelings and strong emotions. The support and encouragement of facilitators and other group members help children gradually change their thoughts, attitudes, feelings, and behavior. In fact, the group can provide a safe, non-judgmental, and supportive testing ground for new kinds of behaviors.

> Jamahl was a friendly, outgoing ten-year-old who always had a ready smile, unless something aroused an uncomfortable feeling in him, such as anger, sadness, embarrassment, or fear. Whenever this happened, Jamahl became very quiet.
>
> After being a member of a support group for awhile, and after hearing others in the group speak about their chemically dependent family members, Jamahl was finally able to talk about his alcoholic mom, whom he hadn't seen for over two years. As Jamahl continued in the support group cycle, it not only became easier for him to talk about his mom, but also about how embarrassed he was and how angry he felt toward her. As Jamahl shared his feelings, many others in the group nodded their heads, and no one laughed.

Support groups can become safe and secure places where youngsters can help one another cope positively with life's complexities.

Benefits of Support Groups

Support groups equip children with skills to take better care of themselves. This is true whether or not children come from homes where chemical dependence is a problem. Youngsters who get help in integrating healthy living skills into their daily lives are far less likely to use or abuse alcohol and other drugs as they grow and develop. Children benefit from support groups that help them:

- develop an understanding about alcohol and other drugs
- understand chemical dependence as a disease
- learn how to identify and express feelings appropriately
- learn a variety of problem-solving strategies and coping skills
- develop a sense of community in which they feel encouraged, affirmed, and nurtured
- overcome feelings of guilt, shame, and isolation
- increase and celebrate self-awareness, self-esteem, and self-worth
- have fun—be children—while achieving other important goals

As school-based support group programs strive to achieve these goals and objectives, they can make an incredible impact on the lives of children. Having a safe place to share feelings, thoughts, and problems frees many youngsters to concentrate more fully on school. The interactions children have with each other—their shared love, encouragement, and support—make support groups richly rewarding experiences for all involved.

Types of Groups

As stated in Chapter 1, we advocate two distinctive types of support groups for elementary schools: *Living Skills* groups and *Concerned Persons* groups. *Living Skills* groups are open to all children who seek to learn more about positive, healthy living skills than an in-class prevention curriculum alone can offer. *Concerned Persons* groups are designed more specifically for children who come from families with chemical dependence and its concurrent problems. Children with a parent, sibling, grandparent, or other relative who is chemically dependent should be encouraged to take part in a *Concerned Persons* group.

Both types of groups share the goals and the many benefits outlined above. Both types of groups foster prevention by teaching children a variety of positive, healthy living skills. For example, a fifthgrader in a *Living Skills* group can find support and help in dealing with the death of a loved one. Another fifth-grader in a *Concerned Persons* group may learn new ways to identify and express his or her feelings. Each type of group offers children both education and support. And both are crucial.

The Living Skills Group

A *Living Skills* group emphasizes health, wellness, and disease prevention, especially the disease of chemical dependence. Any and all youngsters in a school may participate in this group process. In a *Living Skills* group, children discover how to identify and express feelings; they learn important information about alcohol and other drugs and about chemical dependence; they acquire an array of life skills; and they celebrate their own uniqueness.

The children in a *Living Skills* group gain these new awarenesses and personal insights primarily through games and activities. Being involved in the process of a *Living Skills* group helps children to value and treat *themselves,* as well as others, with more dignity and respect.

The central focus of a *Living Skills* group are the core life skills (feeling processing, problem solving, decision making). Children involved in the process of a *Living Skills* group—which generally meets for eight weeks—support and encourage one another to test out their new life skills along the way. All children in a school can benefit from this unique approach to health promotion.

The Concerned Persons Group

Although similar to a *Living Skills* group in teaching children positive, healthy living skills, the central focus of a *Concerned Persons*

21

group is helping children learn to cope with family chemical dependence. Research estimates that one out of every five children is harmfully affected by someone else's (generally, a family member's) chemical dependence. This becomes the common bond of the youngsters in a *Concerned Persons* group.

Since many of these children have never spoken openly about what's going on at home, it generally takes time for them to open up. Initially, therefore, the facilitator builds trust so children are willing to share and discuss their common problems. As the group proceeds—usually meeting for ten weeks—the facilitator helps children develop personal coping strategies. It's inspirational to watch the children as they begin to take good care of themselves.

Although some schools are hesitant about offering *Concerned Persons* groups, fearing parental repercussions or group members being stigmatized, facilitators of *Living Skills* groups often report surprise at the number of group members who identify themselves as coming from families with chemical dependence. To meet the needs of those children, schools often agree to offer *Concerned Persons* groups that adhere to strict confidentiality. Still, some parents—as is their right—refuse to allow their children to participate.

When such is the case, or when *Concerned Persons* groups do not become available in a school, it's important not to give up on establishing support groups. Children from chemically dependent homes can still derive real benefit by participating in *Living Skills* groups. There, they will learn to identify and express feelings, develop essential life skills, and learn that family chemical dependence is not their fault.

Elements of Support Group Design

As we saw with Becky and Jamahl earlier, the children neither opened themselves to their feelings nor to the emotional support of their respective groups by accident. Rather, they felt secure at the group meetings. By the time each disclosed her or his painful feelings, each had realized it was safe and appropriate to do so. Both children came to this realization because the format and conduct of their respective group meetings had established a solid foundation of trust. At each meeting, group facilitators had introduced weekly themes, had woven group members into the process and discussion, and had worked hard to create a safe and secure environment by providing clear rules backed up by consistently enforced consequences.

This section of the chapter outlines the major elements of effective group design. These elements apply to both *Living Skills* groups and to *Concerned Persons* groups. Underlying principles and details of the group process will be laid out step by step in later chapters.

An effective support group for elementary children consists of the following essential elements:

- a skilled and well-trained facilitator(s) to guide the process
- six to ten group members (children), not more than three years apart in age, who faithfully attend and participate
- a regular meeting time
- a regular meeting place that allows for privacy, for confidentiality, and for participants to feel comfortable and at ease
- a meeting structure and format that ensure the children's physical and emotional safety

When these elements are consistent, the group will evolve: nervous children will begin to feel comfortable; quiet and shy youngsters will speak up; all the children will begin to interact with each other and will realize that group can actually be a valuable experience that's filled with learning and fun.

As bonding and trust evolve, the group becomes a safe place where youngsters talk openly about their lives, sometimes sharing secrets they've never talked about before. The children explore a full range of feelings, including anger, happiness, sadness, fear, and joy. Likewise, they learn to take risks as they try out new and healthier ways of relating to others. As intimacy develops, youngsters encourage and support one another so completely that the group meeting can, and often does, become for them one of the most highly anticipated and enjoyable times in their week.

Format for Support Group Meetings

Usually, small group sessions are scheduled weekly and begin with a warm-up activity. After the warm-up, the facilitator introduces the main topic for that week, and the group members engage in one or two creative games or activities that help bring the topic to life. The facilitator then guides the children in a discussion of the topic and how it applies to them. The meeting ends with a closing activity. Generally, a group session lasts from 30 to 60 minutes.

Format of a Group Session

Opening Activity: Check in; warm-up activity

Main Topic: mini-lecture; experiential games or other activities; discussion

Closing Activity: wind-down exercise if necessary; closing ritual.

Opening Activity

Opening activities may include a check-in, a relaxation exercise, or just a brief warm-up question like "Who's your favorite cartoon character?" This provides an opportunity for the facilitator(s) to welcome the children, help them settle in, and give them a chance to participate verbally from the outset. The opening activity helps children focus on the group process and begin to have fun.

Main Topic

The facilitator introduces the main topic of the meeting to the group members. If, for example, the topic is "feelings," the facilitator might introduce it by giving a mini-lecture stressing that everyone has feelings and that all feelings are okay. The children might brainstorm a variety of feelings, list them on the chalkboard, and explore how some of them are more uncomfortable than others. After this discussion, facilitators introduce one or two specially designed games or activities so children can *experience* the main topic. For example, the children might interact with feeling puppets: Angry Amy, Sad Stefano, Happy Harry, Guilty Gamahl, and their friends. Or, they could play a Simon Sez feeling game in which children guess another's secret feeling, followed by the group members talking about the times they've had similar feelings.

After completing these games or activities, the children discuss how this information relates to their lives, and they comment on what they've learned in group. This is education, awareness, and support in action. The children gain personal insights both through information given them and through their interaction with one another. They benefit from listening to others share similar thoughts, feelings, and experiences, and they begin to reveal themselves in the process.

Closing Activity

Group concludes with a brief winding down activity that prepares youngsters to leave the safety of the group. Also, it is very helpful to close the meeting with a *ritual*—a special song, a collective hug, a holding of hands in a circle to pass around a squeeze of energy—to bind the children together. Most groups develop their own special closing ceremony. Effective closings are an essential part of the meeting structure and format that facilitators should observe faithfully.

Dealing with Sensitive Issues

During some group meetings, children will be taking a look at parts of their lives they may rather not explore, like chemically dependent family members, divorced parents, or their own self-defeating behaviors. Far from providing children with a good time, such explorations can be painful for them as they unlock an array of uncomfortable feelings. When a child's tone of voice, body language, or facial expression suggest that he or she is struggling inwardly with difficult feelings, the facilitator may gently ask how or what the child is feeling. It is essential that the facilitator approach such a confrontation gradually, gently, and with deep respect for the dignity and worth of the child. This requires the facilitator to point out whatever can be observed, but never to offer negative criticism, to accuse, or to judge.

Keep in mind that these groups offer education and support, not therapy. It is best to refer children needing therapy to an outside agency. You can expect a certain degree of conflict in the group meetings, and know that it's a positive sign of growing group intimacy. But other issues may not be appropriate for in-depth exploration in a support group setting. Although issues of neglect, abandonment, and some instances of abuse are often discussed fruitfully at group level, many stories of physical and sexual abuse and other traumatic experiences go beyond the scope of group work. Children who have experienced such traumas need the help of professional therapists and counselors. Don't hesitate to refer such children through the proper channels to a qualified professional. Doing so is not a failure on your part, but an excellent, caring practice. Likewise, remember that reporting suspected cases of child abuse is mandated by law. If such an issue should arise in group, be sure to follow your school's reporting procedures.

Starting the First Group 4

So how do you get started? Regard your first support group as a pilot project. Setting it up with care and consideration will lay the foundation for future groups to build on. To begin, you must first obtain the endorsement and backing of the school administration. Remember, the administration controls the school's important resources—space, time, policies, and money. Likewise, facilitators and other teachers in the school need to feel that the administration is behind their efforts. Because administrative approval and support is so critical to the long-term success of a support group program in your school, this topic will be discussed in detail in Chapter 5.

Once you've obtained administrative approval, follow the steps below to start your first support group:

- Determine how large the group will be.
- Decide how best to schedule the group during the school day.
- Establish where the group will meet.
- Choose whether the group should be "open" or "closed."
- Develop means to obtain parental consent.
- Assure group confidentiality.

- Adopt group rules (and consequences).
- Clarify policies on dealing with instances of physical and sexual abuse.

Each of these steps is explained in detail in the sections that follow.

Group Size

Although it takes only a few children to get your first group off the ground, it's important to strike a balance between serving children well and accommodating the number of children who want to participate. (Note: Chapter 8 will discuss the process of recruiting children for the support groups.) Six to ten children provide an optimum number for rich group dynamics and useful interactions. A group of less than four often lacks the energy for good mutual sharing. When the group size extends beyond ten, the level of individual attention and sharing diminishes, and some children are apt to get lost in the shuffle. If you find that more children want to participate, offer more groups as it becomes possible to do so.

Group Scheduling

Elementary support groups meet weekly. This allows children to integrate the insight and support gained from each session without it interfering with their studies and other activities. For consistency, schedule the group for the same day each week. You may meet either during the school day or right after school. We are aware of programs that run quite smoothly and successfully using either format.

Even though scheduling a support group to meet during the school day may conflict with class time, utilizing this format can work to great advantage. A support group that meets during the school day is a more integral part of the curriculum. Although you will want to make the meeting *day* consistent, you may rotate meeting *times* so that children will not miss instruction in the same subject each week. For example, for the first week, schedule the group to meet during the first instructional hour, for the second week, schedule it during the second instructional hour, and so on.

Children participate in group with the proviso that they make up all missed work. Teachers should receive a group schedule every month so that they'll know in advance what class a child will miss and can make arrangements for the child to make up missed school work.

When starting up your very first groups—especially if you have to deal with some resistance to the whole concept of support groups—it may be necessary to schedule the group to meet after school. An after-school group should meet weekly, on a designated day, immediately after school. This group may be looked upon as another after-school activity. If your school offers late bus ("activity bus") transportation for youngsters participating in other after-school activities, getting group members home shouldn't be a problem. Once administrators, teachers, and parents witness positive changes in the lives of young people, it's not uncommon for after-school groups to become integrated into the regular school day.

What's important here is getting started. Use whichever initial scheduling you judge has the most chance for success in your school.

Group Meeting Place

Just as it's important for the group to meet weekly at a designated time, so also is it important that the group meeting be held in the same place each week. The location, size, and decor—the atmosphere—of the group's meeting room are very important in establishing a safe, welcoming space for children to open up and take risks.

Classrooms are undesirable places for group meetings. Generally, they are too large and are filled with too many possible distractions. Ideally, the meeting room needs to be small and cozy, a place where interruptions and potential distractions are minimal. Privacy is essential so youngsters won't be afraid that others outside the room may overhear them. The room must also provide enough space for activities and games. A carpeted floor to sit on is a plus.

Take some time to scout out a good place for your group room. We know that such a space is often at a premium in a school setting, so remember that your most important considerations are privacy and regular availability.

"Open" or "Closed" Group Meetings

Unfortunately, not all children choose to join a support group and not all referrals for group come at the same time. This poses the dilemma of how to accommodate more children once group meetings have begun: Should a group remain "open" to new members, or, once formed, should it remain "closed"? Adding new members to a group in progress seriously compromises (at least temporarily) the trust and intimacy already established within the group. The new member is also at a disadvantage, having missed previous exchanges of information and any bonding that has already occurred. For these reasons, we recommend that you "close" a support group after the second meeting, even if it means that children must wait six to eight weeks for a new group to begin.

Obtaining Parental Consent

Carefully thought out policies and procedures for getting parental consent help a support group maintain its feasibility and integrity. Parental consent policies must consider the children's needs, the parents' rights to privacy, the school's desire to help its students, and the law so as to avoid any legal action being taken against the school.

As alluded to in Chapter 3, parents generally don't mind their children participating in a *Living Skills* group. However, a *Concerned Persons* group is often more problematic, and parental resistance, often under the cloak of denial and fear, frequently comes into play. Likewise, some children resolutely refuse to participate in a *Concerned Persons* group if their parents must be notified.

We suggest that the school mail a letter to the parents of *all* students that:

- describes both a *Living Skills* and a *Concerned Persons* group

- encourages parents to allow their children to receive the services these groups can provide
- informs parents that they must contact the school if they do *not* want their child to participate

(See Example 4.1: Sample Parental Consent Letter, on pages 32 and 33.)

In our experience, chemically dependent parents may refuse to allow their child to participate in a *Concerned Persons* group (perhaps believing that allowing such participation is an admission of their chemical dependence). However, they may let their child take part in a *Living Skills* group because they want their child to acquire the coping skills necessary to ward off potential problems with alcohol and other drugs.

Sometimes you or another school staff member will identify a particular child who could benefit by participating in a support group, but whose parents refuse to allow it. If you've clearly explained the purpose and format of the support groups to the parents and they still don't want their child involved, the best you can do is to refer the child to the school counseling services for individual assistance.

Group Confidentiality

Confidentiality is the cornerstone for making group meetings safe and supportive. To share problems and deep feelings, children must *know* that what they say will be kept in confidence. Children will not open up if they think that what they share will become common knowledge around school. In our experience, children rarely break rules of confidentiality. Staff members must remember their responsibilities as well. Except in cases where the law requires such revelation (if a child is being abused), it is inappropriate for a group facilitator to reveal to others that Willie's dad is an alcoholic, that Janet's mom is currently serving a jail sentence, or that Patrick's parents are both working on their second divorce. Remember, it's a major step

Example 4.1   Sample Parental Consent Letter

Dear Parents:

Alcohol and other drug use is a problem children inevitably confront as they grow and develop. Using these substances can have a significant negative impact on children. Sadly, younger and younger children report that they feel pressure to use alcohol or other drugs. Happily, however, research indicates that children who possess healthy living skills are less likely to become harmfully involved with alcohol and other drugs.

Here at (NAME OF SCHOOL), we're committed to do our part to assist students in dealing with this issue in positive ways. Support groups are one resource available to help students develop a variety of healthy living skills. Two different types of support groups are currently available:

Living Skills Group

Open to all students, this group equips children with basic life skills: identifying, expressing, and taking responsibility for feelings; learning accurate, age-appropriate information about alcohol, other drugs, and chemical dependence; developing problem-solving skills; and feeling good about themselves. This group meets weekly for eight weeks.

Concerned Persons Group

This group is open to any students experiencing difficulties, problems, or concerns as a result of someone else's alcohol or other drug use. It provides students with education about basic life skills and support for coping positively with their difficulties and concerns. This group meets weekly for ten weeks.

These groups meet right after school.

Example 4.1   Sample Parental Consent Letter

—OR—

These groups meet for a single class period once a week. The class period for group rotates regularly, so students miss very little time from any one class. Students are required to make up any missed class work while participating in a support group.

We want to make these valuable resources available to any student who'd like to join. Unless we hear otherwise from you, we'll assume we have your permission for your child to participate.

Please feel free to call (NAME & TELEPHONE NUMBER) if you have any questions or concerns about the support groups and your child's possible participation in them. We treat all information confidentially and respectfully.

Sincerely,

for children to share painful parts of their lives, and they might never trust to share again if such information is circulated to no purpose.

Teachers do have a right to know when a child will miss class due to his or her participation in a support group. However, to help maintain confidentiality, it's a good idea to designate *Living Skills* and *Concerned Persons* groups by colors. For example, call a *Living Skills* group the "Red Group," a *Concerned Persons* group the "Green Group." That way, neither school staff nor anyone else (except specific group members) will know either what kind of group a child is in or what the child's specific problem(s) might be. Teachers will only know that one—or more—of their students is taking part in a support group.

Sometimes a teacher who is particularly concerned about a child's behavior in the classroom will seek additional guidance to help the child. With the child's permission, information and specific strategies may be shared, as appropriate. Such authorized sharing can be beneficial for all concerned, especially for the child.

As mentioned above, the group facilitator *must* break confidentiality in suspected cases of child abuse and make a report to the appropriate authorities. Therefore, when you begin group sessions, inform the children at the very first meeting of this: "If you share in group that someone is hurting you or touching you inappropriately, I have to report that information to help you stay safe."

Group Rules

Bringing together a group of children (some of whom will be new to each other) to create an atmosphere in which they feel safe and willing to share thoughts and feelings is a major undertaking. Many children will have never participated in a group process before, so they will be unaccustomed to the expectations and the boundaries of a support group. Group rules and consequences for violating those rules ensure that all group participants will be safe and treated with the dignity and respect they deserve.

Here are a few guidelines to consider in establishing group rules and consequences.

1. Keep rules to a minimum. The group process itself will take care of most problem areas.

2. Make sure that the group rules are simple so that children understand them clearly.

3. Frame the rules as positive statements. This is important in order to reinforce the goal of imparting positive, healthy living skills and coping strategies. Children hear "No, you can't do that" or "That's not okay" so often they will respond much better to *positive rules* than they will to those that just seem to get them into trouble. For example, "One person talks at a time" is a very different—and a much more positive—rule than "Don't interrupt."

4. Rules need to be consistently enforced. It's vital to follow through with appropriate consequences each time a child violates a rule.

5. Make sure that you can administer the consequences if rules are broken.

The suggested group rules and consequences listed on page 36 might be ones you could establish by following the above guidelines.

Print the rules and consequences on a piece of posterboard and display it in the group meeting room. At the beginning of each group session, review them and make sure the children understand them all. The consistency of this practice helps remind the children that they're safe in group and that the rules serve to protect them.

As we've already seen, the most important rule for any group is confidentiality: "What we say here stays here." Children are more open when they believe that what they share will not be spread around the playground or told to their parents. Make certain the children understand that this rule, as well as all other rules, applies to the group facilitator(s) or leader(s) as well. As you review the rules at the beginning of each group session, always share the exception to

Suggested Group Rules

1. One person talks at a time.
2. Respect each other.
3. Put-ups only.
4. You can pass.
5. What we say here stays here.

Suggested Consequences

Coming to group is like playing baseball—three-strikes and you're out. Each group meeting is like a new time at-bat—it starts with no strikes on any-one. When someone breaks a rule, the group facilitator may give him or her a strike.

Strike One—A warning

Strike Two—A 5- to 10-minute time out

Strike Three—Set up a conference*

the confidentiality rule: "If you share in group that someone is hurt-ing you or touching you inappropriately, I have to report that infor-mation to help you stay safe."

Elementary children rarely violate the confidentiality rule. However, the rule is so important, it must always be stressed and never be compromised.

---

*The purpose of the conference is to determine if the support group best meets the child's needs. The facilitator(s), program coordinator, school coun-selor, child, and parents may attend this meeting. The outcome may be that the child remains in the group, or is asked to meet regularly with the school counselor, or is referred to a community resource, or some combination of these outcomes.

Dealing with Instances of Abuse

Before the first group meeting, learn your school's policy for handling and reporting cases of suspected child abuse. Teachers are mandated by law to report all such suspected cases. Since this can be an emotionally distressing experience, it's helpful to follow established policies and procedures and to activate your own support system.

If a group member is being physically or sexually abused it may come to your attention either directly or indirectly. (Note: You may see more instances in a *Concerned Persons* group, since a positive correlation exists between chemical dependence and child abuse.) As you work with the children in your group, pay attention to a child's exhibiting the following signs, all of which may signal abuse:

- fear of being touched
- unexplainable or oddly placed bruises
- consistent wearing of jackets, long-sleeve shirts, and long pants—regardless of the temperature
- excessive fearfulness for or protectiveness of younger siblings
- undue fear of parents or other adults
- exhibiting inappropriate seductive or sexual behavior

Always trust your instincts. If a group participant discloses information during a session, or if your suspicions become aroused for other reasons, ask to meet privately with the child to explore your concerns. It's better to question the child and be wrong than never to ask. Although group is not the appropriate place to explore the individual circumstances of abuse, you can let the children know that abuse is a serious matter and that you will take action on it.

If you do meet individually with a child, let the child know that he or she is not in trouble and that you care very much about his or her well-being and safety. Be careful, however, not to make promises you can't keep: "This will never happen again." Obtain the basic facts about the abuse and connect the child with the school social worker, counselor, nurse, or whoever handles such matters at your school. Accompany the child to see this person and—whenever possible—stay with the child for the first meeting.

Final Steps

This chapter has explored the important "nuts and bolts" issues or steps necessary to start your first group. As you progress, keep these three suggestions in mind:

1. *Proceed slowly.* Remember, the policies and procedures you develop now are laying the foundation for the future.

2. *Get all the help you can.* Work in conjunction with the school administration and other key staff so that they can assist and support you.

3. *Celebrate your accomplishments along the way.* Celebration will energize you and give you the enthusiasm you'll need to continue this important process.

Developing a Support Group Program

5

Very often the insight, vision, and hard work of only one or two educators gets an initial support group started. When the excitement and momentum generated by that group spreads to other students, school staff, and the broader community, and when this enthusiasm, in turn, leads to increased backing from school administrators, parents, and referral agencies, and to more acceptance from the children, you'll find yourself needing a support group *program.* Setting up an entire program takes further planning. This chapter details the administrative structure, organization, and logistics of a support group program that is composed of more than one group.

Remember, you gave a lot of thoughtful time, consideration, and planning to getting your first group started. The same care must be given to create a program that can serve an increased number of children in an organized and effective manner. This chapter describes the process of successfully developing a support group program.

Three basic ingredients are necessary to accommodate successfully the many children who can benefit from support groups:

1. *Group Facilitators or Leaders.* An efficient program will need an ever-growing pool of educators and other interested people

from which to draw and train leaders to facilitate groups as needs arise. A strong pool of potential leaders allows *Living Skills* and *Concerned Persons* groups to run concurrently throughout the school year. (Note: Chapters 6 and 7 will explain how to recruit and train support group leaders.)

2. *A Program Coordinator.* This individual manages the process of recruiting, training, and supervising group leaders, scheduling and overseeing all support groups, and meeting with newly referred youngsters. The program coordinator also coordinates the communication network with the school administration network, teachers, parents, students, and the wider community.

3. *Patience.* Successfully establishing a school-based support group program doesn't happen overnight. It is a significant task that requires significant commitment, time, and energy.

A Typical Program's Evolution

It takes time for support group programs to evolve. Most begin with the commitment and dedication of a few educators who want to make a difference in the lives of their students. One educator who initiated such a process recently told us, "I went 'fishing' to help a few students who were hurting. While this worked well, it took a couple of years before I realized that I had actually caught a 'whale.'" When beginning, remember to be patient and to allow things to grow naturally. Here's how one support group program developed over time.

Two teachers noticed that many students responded positively to an in-class prevention curriculum. Some youngsters asked for more information, but there wasn't time to address all their questions and concerns. Other children, through tears, hanging heads, isolation, and comments about alcohol and other drugs, made it painfully clear that their lives were probably touched by chemical dependence. Responding to a lack of available resources, the two teachers took steps to initiate a support group.

After securing the principal's okay and enlisting the support of the counseling staff, the teachers attended some workshops on preventing chemical dependence and on facilitating support groups in the school setting. Equipped with new insights and information, the teachers developed a basic group format and began the first weekly support group (an after-school group, since it posed the fewest problems to getting started). The school counselor and nurse referred a handful of children. To the surprise of the group leaders, the children responded very well and opened up to the process. Group quickly became a real force in the children's lives. For many, the day of the group meeting became their favorite day of the week. Slowly but surely, more children asked to participate in the program.

In the program's second year, the school provided in-service training on chemical dependence and co-dependence and their impact on children in the classroom. A staff training session also explored the stresses and pressures that youngsters face today that put many children at high risk for emotional and psychological problems. During the in-service training, group leaders described to other staff members how the support group operated and benefited the children. Using brief personal (anonymous) vignettes about two children in previous groups, a letter, and some of the children's drawings, the leaders dramatically illustrated the impact the group had. At a parents' evening, the group leaders and the school counselor discussed raising healthy children and talked about the support group program. Soon, there were far too many children to be served in a single group, so the leaders offered two support groups. The leaders recruited a third teacher, who received on-the-job training by co-leading a group. Still more referrals came in. These served as needs assessments for expanding the program even further. By the end of the second year, four after-school groups were being offered, on two separate days.

In the program's third and fourth years, five educators and interested community professionals received support group facilitation training. With groups operating three, then four, days a week after school, a program coordinator was appointed. The PTA and local civic groups began helping to fund the program. Realizing the incredible benefits, administrators made support groups an integral part of the school day, rather than simply an after-school program.

As you can see, this program's growth was steady and strong, but it required a lot of work. It's one thing to lead an effective support group and quite another to create a solid program. Sometimes you'll encounter discouraging obstacles. That's why it's important to be patient and allow the process to evolve over time. Keep in mind that quality groups will clearly demonstrate both a positive impact and that increasing numbers of youngsters need them. Seeing this helps even the most hesitant and resistant school staff recognize how essential such a program is to the school's well-being.

If you want to build such a program in your school, follow these successive steps:

1. Obtain administrative approval.
2. Appoint a program coordinator.
3. Build a school team.
4. Build a community team.
5. Promote the program.

Obtaining Administrative Approval

As we saw briefly in Chapter 4, securing the school administration's approval and support is the first step in developing and implementing a successful support group program. Without administrative approval and assistance, a program simply cannot exist, let alone grow and flourish. Before you approach administration, however, it's often helpful to enlist the support of the school's counseling staff. They are probably all too familiar with the significant problems in students' lives that are the result of chemical dependence. Most counseling staffs will gladly welcome the idea of a support group program and want to play a key role in the process. Look also to the school nurse and school secretary for support. These are "front-line" people who are often the first to encounter the many problems students experience. Having the support of these staff members will make it easier to approach the principal and other administrative staff with your plan.

Spend time in careful thought and preparation before attempting to garner administrative approval. With the help of the allies mentioned above, develop a concisely-written proposal that explicitly delineates the following 3 P's:

1. the *problem,* particularly its scope and extent

2. the *plan* to ameliorate the problem

3. the *positives* to be derived from putting the plan into action

Comprehensive homework in each of these areas will result in a well-written and persuasive proposal.

The Problem: Understanding It

Begin by getting the facts. Just how many students are affected by familial chemical dependence? How many youngsters come from divorced families? What is the incidence of child abuse today? What's the average age children begin to experiment with alcohol and other drugs? These are important questions for you to answer and to answer with hard and accurate data.

You can find such data by speaking with a professional from the local mental health center, government agency, university, or by referring to the facts listed in Chapter 2 of this book. Likewise, check with your own school district to see if it has already gathered such data. Let people know what you're doing and solicit their support. They might be able to provide additional information from their own experience concerning the effects of chemical dependence on local children. The Children's Defense Fund, the National Association for Children of Alcoholics, and similar groups can give you important information and can serve as links to people or organizations who have organized programs similar to the one you want to establish.

You don't have to re-invent the wheel. There's support available to help you get started (see Appendix C for a listing of national resources). Your proposal needs to present clearly the problems children face today and to show how they interfere with the children's learning at school.

The Plan: Explaining What the Program Looks Like

Make sure your proposal tells what you are going to do. State how many support groups will be offered per week, their formats, who will be leading them, and how the leaders will be trained. Include also the number of students that will be in a group, how they will be selected (see Chapter 8), and how many hours of staff time will be necessary per week to do an adequate job of organizing and leading the groups. Spell out everything as clearly as you can and try not to leave any critical questions unanswered.

The Positives: Describing the Benefits of the Program

Persuasively describe how the program will benefit the school and community. Recount how youngsters who learn and continue to practice positive, healthy life skills will feel better about themselves, will perform better at school, and will be less likely to get into serious trouble either in school or in the community. Explain that children who go through the program will also be less likely to use alcohol and other drugs as they get older. Point out that learning specific coping strategies in *Concerned Persons* groups will help children take better care of themselves.

Check out existing support group programs and ask about the benefits they've noted. Generally, you'll find reports of better attendance, grades, and attitudes, along with a reduction in behavior problems. Point out how school staffs are helped by their students' developing more positive attitudes about learning. Staff members will feel good about referring students to support groups that really work.

Good support groups can free up classroom teachers to do what they do best—teach.

Presenting a proposal that pays attention to each of the above three areas will go a long way to securing administrative approval and support.

Appointing a Program Coordinator

When two or three support groups are up and running, it's time to select a program coordinator who will be responsible for supervising every phase of the program's operation and for maintaining quality control. More specifically, the coordinator's responsibilities include recruiting, training, supervising group leaders, scheduling the time and frequency of groups, assigning facilitators and children to groups, providing continuing in-service training for staff, and developing a communication network both inside and outside of school to foster greater support and awareness. This is no small task. Thus, the program coordinator must be a person who has the time and the "know how" to get things done smoothly and efficiently.

If the individual is selected from among existing school staff, he or she must be free from at least half of his or her "regular" job responsibilities. If you decide to hire someone from outside the school, try to find someone who has previous experience in an educational setting. Someone who has coordinated youth support groups in the community might be an attractive candidate. To repeat an essential point, the program coordinator needs adequate time and resources to get the job done. The responsibility requires at least a half-time position and should *never* be tacked onto a person's full-time job.

Building a School Team

A support group program always benefits from having allies on the school staff. A "school team" can support the program's growth and development in many ways. It is a source of potential group facilitators (see Chapters 6 and 7 on selecting and training group leaders) and key program advocates. Staff allies help break staff resistance by speaking first-hand about the program's positive impact on individual students. Staff in-service sessions also help teachers learn about the pressures students face today, particularly those pressures related to parental chemical dependence. Having a clearer understanding of the purpose and function of groups encourages staff to make referrals. When a teacher sees a positive change in a student whom he or she has referred to the program, the teacher's interest and confidence in the program grows.

A support group program can never have too much staff (faculty) support. Staff backing assures a program long life and protects a program from becoming either one person's private preserve or too dependent on only one or two staff members. With a school team behind it, a support program becomes the *school's* program, is able to sustain itself, and assures itself of readily available leaders to provide services for children in the future.

Building a Community Team

The ideal support group program reaches beyond the school walls to establish strong ties with the larger community. It's not wise to limit a program's operation to school staff only. Remember, chemical dependence has many roots, and the solution to the problem requires a multi-faceted effort. Strong programs actively build support from the community and also help spark other prevention efforts in the community.

Many citizens are just as concerned about prevention issues as are school staff: interested and worried parents who want to help, helping professionals who will gladly lend a hand, and volunteer organizations that are looking to put their resources into worthy projects. Inviting the community to participate in your school's program will add invaluable personal, parental, professional, and financial resources. For example, seek out youth workers as potential group facilitators or co-leaders (see Chapters 6 and 7). Your program can also utilize child therapists, community social workers, clergy, coaches, and scout leaders as group leaders. These people will not only add to your pool of leaders, but will also become community advocates for the program. Likewise, don't forget chemical dependence professionals, who often make excellent candidates in this regard.

Finally, your program will also benefit from community input through a greater awareness of community referral services. With time, the community can become a primary referral resource for new children entering the program.

Promoting the Program—Public Relations and Publicity

If you have a good thing going, don't be bashful. Spread the good word. The community hears often enough about the pervasiveness and devastation caused by chemical abuse. Give them some good news. Tell them about your program's solutions. Offer the community some renewed hope.

A good program always devotes energy to informing the public about itself. Make presentations to the PTA, to local civic groups, and to foundations. Share testimonials of parents, teachers, professionals, and especially children that spell out the program's value. Nothing is more touching or powerful than to hear children speak about how the program has helped them. You can share these messages without betraying confidentiality. For example, plan to display an exhibit of anonymous work (essays, art, poems) that children have created in group. Invite the community to view the exhibit at school, or see if you can arrange to have the exhibit presented at a local mall or community center. Encourage the local press and other media to do a story about the exhibit and the program. As more people come to appreciate your program's value, they'll want to lend their support.

Ensuring a support group program's success and longevity takes dedicated teamwork. Healthy programs reach out for community support by inviting talented, committed individuals to lend a hand.

Selecting Potential Group Leaders

6

Although this chapter is directed to support group program coordinators and organizers (unlike the rest of the book, which is directed to group leaders and leaders-in-training), it focuses on issues that are valuable and important to anyone who wants to work as a group leader with elementary children. If you are a program coordinator, this chapter will help you get a competent and trainable staff together. If you are a group leader or potential group leader, you can learn a lot here that will help you do a better job.

Once a school or school system has made the decision to proceed with a comprehensive support group program, it is incumbent upon program staff to work effectively and competently. A program is only as effective as those who work with the children week after week in the *Living Skills* or the *Concerned Persons* groups. That is why it's important to recruit competent, compassionate people who are consciously working on their own growth and who are interested in and have some knowledge about chemical dependence. In the best programs, the entire staff shares in the responsibility of finding suitable new staff members.

People who work in programs for children have a challenging and responsible opportunity to make a difference. For some of the children in your support groups, the group leader may be the first person in whom they are able to confide their feelings, the first adult who has really listened to them or treated them as worthwhile persons. This is a heavy responsibility, even for an experienced therapist, and can move the best of us off center at times.

Successfully selecting effective group facilitators involves three, equally important elements:

- clarity about the qualities desirable in group leaders
- knowledge about where and how to look for likely candidates
- a workable and effective process for assessing candidates' qualifications and likelihood of success

By paying attention to these three factors, you will be able to recruit a group of competent, compassionate people who can make a great difference in the lives of children.

Qualities Desired in Group Leaders

Our experience has shown us seven categories of desirable qualities to look for in potential group leaders:

- love and empathy for children
- commitment and motivation
- interactive skills
- self-understanding and awareness
- additional psychological factors
- knowledge of chemical dependence or willingness to acquire it
- intangible qualities

Know from the start that no single person will completely possess all the characteristics outlined here. On the surface, in fact, some people may exhibit but a few. Therefore, it's important for you to assess *potential* or *hidden* qualities as well as those that are obvious. Though not an easy task, it is one that can be richly rewarding.

Love and Empathy for Children

Love has many meanings. We use it here to mean a willing intention to further and facilitate the emotional and spiritual growth of another or others. Empathy is the ability to feel or experience what another is feeling. Love and empathy are essential qualities for potential group leaders. Unfortunately, it is not always easy to ascertain their presence uncontaminated by compulsive concern to do what appears right or by needs for self-aggrandizement. So, as you evaluate these factors, remember we all have certain aspects of our personality that are not totally healthy and that none of us is perfect. In looking for love and empathy in others, you're dealing with relative qualities, not absolutes.

Given all this, you obviously want to find people who are basically kind to children, who can give them verbal and non-verbal warmth and appropriate affection. Thoughtfulness, consideration, and an even temper are critical qualities of the persons you seek. Certain questions can help you make determinations regarding the presence of such qualities in potential group leaders and facilitators:

- What kind of relationship do you have with your own children?
- What principles do you use in dealing with children for whom you are responsible?
- What bugs you about children?
- What do you like most about children?
- What aspect of dealing with children makes you most uncomfortable?
- What aspect of dealing with children is most gratifying to you?

On the one hand, you don't want someone who pities children or tries to do much for them. On the other hand, you don't want someone who is trying to fulfill his or her own dependency needs through children.

Sometimes it's not easy to identify the qualities of love and empathy in a potential group leader before he or she actually begins the facilitating work. Then what you should look for in a person who applies to your program is the level of emotional support he or she possesses. The more emotional support a person has, the more likely it is that he or she is approaching the task of facilitating for healthy reasons.

Commitment and Motivation

It is critical to select people who are sincerely interested in support group work with children. Children know almost immediately if adults aren't sincere and interested, if they aren't "real."

In our experience, most group leaders originally apply because working with children is something they really want to do. Some applicants had previous experience working with children, and some did not. Some came on their own (usually a strong indicator of commitment and motivation), and others were encouraged to "try out" by a program director or other group leaders who knew them as friends or colleagues. Many of the most gifted and effective group leaders began with no training and with little or no previous experience. Some of these people were either recovering persons themselves or had experienced chemical dependence in a close family member, and this "tie" was the strongest part of their initial commitment and motivation. Others had no previous experience with chemical dependence but did have a strong desire to work with children.

Motivation and commitment are sometimes difficult to assess, but if the obligations incumbent in the training program are carefully spelled out, and if the applicant does not balk at them, you can be pretty sure that the candidate is willing to carry through.

Interactive Skills

If a potential group leader is a member of the school faculty, you, as program coordinator, may already know something about his or her interactive skills. Consider the candidate's reputation with the students, how he or she works with other teachers, how he or she deals with problems, how he or she handles conflict in the classroom.

Sometimes, particularly for non-teacher, parent, and other prospects who have not been previously required to use interactive skills, information like that mentioned above may be harder to obtain or may be unavailable. However, this alone is not a sufficient reason for rejecting such candidates.

Self-understanding and Awareness

Intellectual and emotional honesty are essential attributes for all candidates. Is the candidate able to say "I don't know" and to acknowledge some of his or her insecurity or anxiety about being part of the program? Education begins when the right questions are asked, and the honest person will ask more about how things work and about what he or she doesn't know or understand. This type of candor is very reassuring.

Many people who are themselves in recovery from chemical dependence, co-dependence, workaholism, or abuse are engaged in processes that greatly enhance their self-understanding and awareness. These people are good prospects for becoming group leaders. However, as a rule of thumb, we suggest that you do not consider anyone who has not completed at least *two years* of recovery—and we encourage you to assess everyone completely. Recovery *per se* does not necessarily guarantee an effective group leader.

Additional Psychological Factors

A number of other psychological factors play a role in a candidate's suitability as a children's support group leader:

- Is the candidate uncomfortable expressing feelings?
- Does the candidate exhibit psychological defenses that might be overly powerful?
- Does the candidate seem unaware how past life, in particular childhood, can influence his or her behavior, especially when it comes to reacting to stressful situations?
- Did the candidate grow up in a home where there was chemi-

cal dependence? Where there was a workaholic? Where there was physical, sexual, mental, or spiritual abuse?

If you find that a candidate answers yes to one or more of these questions, realize that these are all red flags that you must heed in your selection process.

With regard to a candidate's childhood experiences, know that a history of physical or sexual abuse does not automatically eliminate him or her from becoming a facilitator. But know, too, that people with latent or unresolved abuse issues can have a lot of difficulty in leading a group. If a candidate's childhood was troubled and he or she minimizes its importance or seems to have done little to deal with it as it affects his or her present feelings and behavior, be cautious.

Knowledge of Chemical Dependence or Willingness to Acquire It

Again, here is where a recovering person may bring added richness to the group process, due to his or her own personal history and to the additional knowledge he or she has acquired during the recovery process. At the same time, many people who are not recovering themselves have knowledge about chemical dependence or are willing to acquire it. As in recovery, willingness goes a long way toward solving many a teaching or educational dilemma. Perhaps a person has experience with the 12-Step process of AA or Al-Anon, or has had a family member in recovery from chemical dependence or other compulsive disorder, or has taken course work in chemical dependence. These experiences are likely to give you a candidate who has more than average knowledge about chemical dependence. "Street wisdom" is often difficult to access, but some non-chemically dependent people have learned a lot of helpful knowledge from friends or peers that can be put to good use in working with children.

Intangible Qualities

Some candidates possess helpful qualities that are real but resist being pinned down or easily named. Pied pipers are everywhere, folks who possess almost "magical" qualities and who may not have had the right opportunity to express them fully. These are people who work beautifully with children right from the start, and no one can explain why they are so successful. These people exude trustworthiness, and children pick up on that. People whose fears are confined to *real* and appropriate stimuli usually come across this way, and children find them very comfortable to be with. Those who are fearful most of the time radiate that feeling and make children uncomfortable. The former are treasures and will surely enrich your program.

Where to Look for Group Leaders

The first place to look for group leaders is among the school staff. But don't confine your search to teachers only. There may be administrative people, clerical workers, and housekeeping personnel who are effective with children and who would be thrilled to have the chance to work in this type of program. So, publicize your need throughout the entire school staff.

In the community, look to clergy and others involved in church or synagogue work, to recovering people from groups like AA, Al-Anon, and other 12-Step programs, to mental health counselors and family therapists, to your own PTA, and, once your program is started, to your group leaders' friends and colleagues.

Good leaders often come from unlikely places. In one community-based program, hospital personnel from outside the chemical dependence field, family therapy interns, physicians, parents of children in the support group program, and others all proved helpful and effective group leaders. An honest and healthy desire to do the work and a willingness to stay at it seems to be among the most desirable traits of potential leaders. Two notes of caution: (1) It is usually not a good idea to have a parent facilitate a group in a school program in which his or her own child is enrolled; (2) Don't have people new to recovery as group leaders. These people may hear about your program at one of their own recovery meetings and be very attracted to the idea and want distraction. As mentioned previously, wait until recovering people are at least two years along. Both you and they will be glad you did.

The Assessment Process

Once you have identified your candidates, you need to evaluate their strengths and weaknesses and decide whether or not to accept them into your training program. If possible, don't do this alone. Enlist the help of group leaders, school administrators, members of the school counseling staff, and, in an informal way, the children who have been part of the support group program for a while.

Those who help with the interviewing should be well briefed and familiarized with an informative interview process. Perhaps the program coordinator can have a training session for those who will be helping with the interviewing. In the session, emphasize the importance of listening, keeping and looking for eye contact, presenting real or simulated conflict situations for the prospect to respond to. In fact, in the training session, it's a good idea to employ one or two simulated (programmed) candidates that the other staff members can "interview." It is important that interviewers remember that you're all looking for leadership strengths—present and potential—and qualities (as detailed above) rather than a lot of knowledge and experience in chemical dependence or small group work. Finally, explain to the staff that you are asking them to join you in interviewing not to save you time, but to provide more opportunities for candidates to deal with a group—and, perhaps, a "stressful" group—situation.

Prior to interviewing candidates, ask them to complete an information questionnaire like the one provided in this book. (See Example 6.1: Questionnaire for Prospective Group Facilitators, on pages 58 and 59.) You can use the information the candidate provides to help you plan for the interview and during the interview itself.

When you interview a candidate, emphasize the qualities you're looking for in a group leader, but also acknowledge that no one has them all and that gaining skill in group leadership is a real on-the-job process. During the interview, you might offer some simulated "conflict-of-behavior" situations for the prospect to respond to. Notice eye contact and how well the candidate tracks during the interview. Share one or two of your difficulties with children to see how the candidate responds. Explore the prospect's previous experience with children and any troubles he or she spontaneously recalls or reports. If the candidate is a parent, you might probe his or her parenting style and ask for kinds of problems the prospect has had with his or her own children. This "personalized" question, by the way, may be the most important one you can ask a candidate.

As soon as possible after an interview, you and other interviewers should meet to evaluate the process and the candidate. Using an interview checklist like the one found in this book can be a valuable tool to help everyone focus on the dynamics of the process and on the qualities of the candidate. (See Example 6.2: Interview Checklist, on pages 60 and 61.)

Even though the interview is a valuable tool in selecting good people, be sure to solicit and use references as well. It's always valuable to obtain information from those who have worked with and known the prospect over a period of time. If a candidate is someone you've worked with and you feel you know, it's still a good idea to get input from others who know him or her. This includes input from the person's peers and, if the candidate is a member of the school staff, from children in the school.

You may be alerted to serious problems by the candidate himself or herself, by speaking with others about the candidate, or through the candidate's references. If necessary, ask the candidate for additional information, seek further references, or probe gently for more details. The thing to trust in all this is your intuition. If you sense anything that raises red flags—serious questions in your mind—*pay attention to your feelings.*

In addition to obvious problems like a personal history of violent behavior, stay alert for either of the following two issues:

Example 6.1   Questionnaire for Prospective Group Facilitators

Name _____

Address_____

Telephone   home: _____ work: _____

1. Why do you want to work as a facilitator of children's support groups?

2. What previous experience (work, play, home) do you have that you feel might be helpful in this work?

3. What is your own personal or family experience with chemical dependence or other types of dysfunctional family patterns?

4. Have you ever had any course work, seminars, or other formal learning experiences related to chemical dependence?

5. Do you have children of your own? If so, give sexes and ages and any experience with them that might be helpful to you in your role as a group facilitator.

Example 6.1   Questionnaire for Prospective Group Facilitators

6. If you have children, what is the most troublesome problem you have in your relationship with them? If you have no children, what is the most difficult thing about your relationship with your parents?

7. Describe one or two of your most important growth experiences.

8. What do you do to take care of yourself or to celebrate yourself?

9. Describe your personal support system.

Example 6.2   Interview Checklist

Candidate's Name: _____

Apparent motivation and commitment:

Reservations expressed about doing this work:

Knowledge or experience
- healthy living skills
- work with children
- child development
- chemical dependence
- co-dependence

Love and empathy for children

Enthusiasm

Comfort with displaying and expressing feelings

Self-understanding and awareness of personal issues

Awareness of personal biases

Support system

Example 6.2   Interview Checklist

Personal warmth

Ability to have fun

Personal creativity

Unusual or additional qualities or competencies

Interactive skills during the interview
- listening ability
- clarity of communication
- conciseness
- non-verbal communication

Fearfulness

Warning signs

****

Candidate's apparent strengths:

Candidate's apparent weaknesses:

Issues or potential problems requiring further exploration:

- the candidate's being a victim of physical or sexual abuse
- any patterns—including co-dependence—arising from the candidate's being a child from a dysfunctional (chemically dependent, workaholic, excessively authoritarian, or excessively permissive) home

Physical or Sexual Abuse

Whether or not a candidate has ever been the victim of physical or sexual abuse is a key factor because people with unresolved or unidentified abuse issues can have great difficulty leading groups. Such people often have trouble being "present"—concentrating on the task at hand. They may also have problems with boundaries that can seriously interfere with healthy group process. For example, they may be either more affectionate or more distant with the children than is appropriate, or they may come to use one or more of the children as personal confidants.

As you are probably aware, it is not easy to assess the matter of abuse—especially sexual abuse—since people may not even be aware that they were abused as children. If, however, a candidate's questionnaire, interview, or references provide indications of high levels of anxiety, bizarre dreams in which abuse is threatened or occurs, a sense of personal shame that permeates large segments of the person's life, self-mutilation, low self-esteem, or "fantasies" of abuse having occurred during childhood, you can generally trust them as indicators that the person has been the victim of some sort of abuse. Likewise, a person's verbal responses, body language, and non-verbal behavior can all provide valuable clues to dysfunction, anxiety, shame, and fear that can have their roots in abuse.

As we've seen earlier, being the victim of abuse does not necessarily exclude a candidate from being a group leader if the person has resolved the abuse issues through appropriate means (counseling or therapy). If you are unsure about a candidate, know that the training process will provide a period for him or her to function as an observer in a small group (see Chapter 7). This will give you time to observe the candidate "on the job," as it were, and additional time to assess the issue of his or her suitability for being a support group leader.

History of a Dysfunctional Home

If a candidate grew up in a troubled or highly stressful home, he or she may have problems with control and caretaking behaviors, which, when excessive, can seriously interfere with a small group's process, play, spontaneity, happiness, and growth. Someone with such a history should not consider being a group leader unless he or she is at least two years along in a recovery process himself or herself.

In conclusion, you should be aware of other personality traits that are legitimate causes for concern. These traits include violent behavior, repressed anger, inability to express feelings, excessive teasing of others, and acting as a victim. It has been our experience, however, that people with these traits usually do not often present themselves as candidates for group leaders. Rather, people who have the desired qualities mentioned earlier are much more apt to apply.

By following the guidelines in this chapter, you will find qualified candidates who generally need only to be involved in an effective training process. That process is outlined in Chapter 7.

The Training Process 7

L eading either *Living Skills* or *Concerned Persons* groups
requires a combination of knowledge and skills. Comfort with
working with children, lesson planning ability, knowing how to use
educational objectives, and a working knowledge of child development comprise one group of competencies with which most school
teachers are quite familiar. Knowledge of and experience with chemical dependence and co-dependence and recovery skills combine to
form another group of competencies that are more familiar to professionals working in the recovery field. It is the task of the training
program to meld these two groups of competencies and to make
them available both to elementary teachers and to professionals from
the recovery community—the two most likely sources of prospective
group leaders—as well as to other group leader candidates, all to the
benefit and affectionate care of children.

Most of this chapter is devoted to outlining the structure and
process of an in-house training program that we have found practical
and effective over the past eight years. However, this training program has always benefited from an experienced person or persons at
its helm. Therefore, we recommend that prospective group leaders

in all start-up programs and in most programs in the first years of development seek training in an established training center. (See Appendix C for a list of National Resources, many of whom offer training opportunities.) We realize that local resources may not always permit this; nevertheless, when feasible, we highly recommend it.

Training Manual

Following the program described in this chapter might prove more beneficial if you provide participants with a training manual. This is not to say that a training manual is a necessity, but it can be a big help. Employing the information in this chapter, you can fashion such a tool. Design the manual to be loose leaf so that you'll be able to revise it with ease. The manual should be long enough to be useful, but not so long as to be intimidating. The manual will be for *your* program, so tailor it to fit and to contain the particular information *you* need. To get you started, however, we offer an example of a usable training manual in Appendix D.

Phases of Training

Know that the sequence and timing of the training phases described in the following pages is an ideal one. The reality can vary widely. Ideally, everyone in the program should be afforded periods of observation and apprenticeship time before having to strike out as full-fledged co-leaders. But if your school is just starting a program, or if your school is small and not many people have expressed an initial interest in participating as group leaders, you—as a potential leader—many find yourself attending an orientation and planning session one day and leading a group the next. Conversely, if people show a lot of interest in a new program, you may find it necessary to begin several new group leaders simultaneously. When we started our first program, we led groups alone for two years. Now, even though our program is well-established, sometimes staffing is thin. Participation will wax and wane. Finally, if you're a "Lone Ranger" and want to start a program, pursue training from an outside source (see Appendix C). Begin where you can. Build and grow as it becomes possible.

An ideal program should have three clearly differentiated training phases:

- Phase One: Observation and Orientation
- Phase Two: Apprenticeship
- Phase Three: Co-leadership or Leadership

Some training program participants might have previously participated in training elsewhere (most of which are extensive, lasting three or four days), while other participants may have to begin group work after only a brief in-house orientation session. For the former group, you may be able to shorten the observation and orientation phase.

Phase One: Observation and Orientation

In this first phase of training, the trainee participates in the play aspects of a group, while simultaneously observing what's going on in the group. The trainee follows all rules set out for all members of the group and actively participates—as if he or she were one of the children—in each session. This does not mean that the trainee cannot assume the role of a helper during a session in order to assist a child or children or that he or she can't practice learning how to set up certain exercises. However, to the extent that this interferes with the trainee getting a sense of what it's like to be a child in one of the groups, such "facilitation" is non-productive.

In addition to involving the trainee in a "walk in another's shoes" sort of exercise, the initial period of training enables the trainee to gain valuable insight by giving him or her time to get in touch with his or her own childlike nature. This, in turn, allows the trainee to proceed with any healing outside of group that may be necessary to be a more comfortable and effective group facilitator. During this phase, the support group leader (the experienced facilitator and "trainer") treats the trainee like any other group member, asking the trainee to disclose feelings, take part in activities and games, produce and describe art work, or talk about what it was like in his or her family.

Using a training manual during this phase can be helpful. We have led trainees through this phase with and without a manual and cannot say that one way is necessarily better than the other. It is, however, very helpful for the trainee to keep a log of observations and feelings. The log can be a valuable adjunct to the feedback and supervisory time the trainee spends with the trainer. Such debriefing time needs to be provided after most sessions so that the leader and the trainee can discuss what went on and can deal with pertinent questions.

Ideally, the length of phase one training should last for eight to ten group sessions, that is, for one cycle of sessions that may extend over a period of two to three months. Again, this is an ideal time-length for this phase, and we realize that your local situation may dictate otherwise.

Phase Two: Apprenticeship

During the second phase, the trainee shares in facilitating a support group along with a more experienced leader. If your program is large enough, the more experienced leader should ideally be a different "preceptor" than in the first phase. This is not a requirement for effective training, but we recommend it where possible.

In phase two, the trainee leaves the participant role he or she assumed in phase one and becomes an assistant leader in group. While directed and assisted by the more experienced group leader, the trainee assumes responsibility and active leadership for at least one activity per group session. As in phase one, debriefing after each session is an extremely important part of the training. The questions and statements below speak to issues that might be explored in a typical debriefing:

- Why did you handle a particular situation the way you did?
- Would it have worked better if I had done this or that?

- I really felt sad when Tim was taking about his parents.
- How could I have led the discussion on defenses more effectively?
- Do you think you were trying to rescue Sarah during the little fight she had with Roberto?

Note that questions and statements like these might be initiated by either party in the debriefing.

We have noted that due either to other pressing responsibilities or to feelings of discomfort, both trainer and trainee tend to want to skip debriefing. *Resist this tendency,* particularly if feelings surfaced during the group session. Remember that the purpose of all this work is to further your own growth and self-realization. To ignore important feelings, whether they be emphatic ones, angry ones, or other forms of discomfort, is to ignore an opportunity for individual growth as well as a chance to become a better group leader. You can't ask children to express feelings openly and honestly if you don't do the same. To foster the debriefing process, we offer Example 7.1: Checklist for Debriefing (on page 70). Use this checklist when you meet for debriefing.

The amount of time spent in phase two varies with the program and available resources. Generally, however, phase two is longer than phase one. Apprenticeship should last six to nine months, a span of time that includes group work on approximately a weekly basis. Again, as noted previously, local demands may alter this time period.

Phase Three: Co-leadership or Leadership

As in phase two, it's a good idea for the trainee to work with a different person (experienced leader) during this phase. The budding facilitator is now a co-leader and shares equal responsibility for the activities and progress of the group. We realize that in some programs you may not have a chance to function as a co-leader after the apprenticeship phase; you may be it—*the leader.* For many talented people this situation is okay. However, whenever possible, it is far more preferable to have co-leaders for all groups.

Example 7.1   Checklist for Debriefing

What feelings did you experience—anger, joy, fear, shame?

Were there any problems with the group process? What were they?

What growth did you observe during the session?

What did you observe and learn about yourself?

What was the most difficult and the most enjoyable thing about this group session?

Whether co-leader or sole leader, you are now responsible for all of the following:

- planning the group sessions
- deciding on many, if not all, of the group's activities
- tracking the children's progress
- making evaluative statements at the conclusion of every session or two
- identifying the kind of behavioral problems that may require individual therapy or other referrals
- managing intra-group conflict when it emerges
- helping the withdrawn, quiet, or frightened child

In this phase of training, you are also responsible to seek out the aid of a supervisor after every second or third group session and schedule a debriefing time. That supervisor may be your co-leader. However, if you and your co-leader are at comparable levels of training, development, and experience, your supervisor needs to be someone else. We cannot emphasize enough the *necessity* for and the *value* of debriefing. (Again, see Example 7.1: Checklist for Debriefing, on page 70.)

Chapter 10 will discuss the significance of *group* supervision and support. We want to say here, however, that you also need and deserve the *individual* guidance and support of a good supervisor. If you get stuck, you need to know it. If you need help, you deserve to get it. If you rate praise, you deserve to get that, too.

Phase three has no time limit. Once you have entered this phase, you are a working facilitator. The support and supervision outlined above should continue as long as you are working with children in groups. Like all forms of good adult education, the learning begun in this training process should continue and will continue, enhanced and enriched by the input you can bring to it from your experience as a group leader.

Areas of Special Emphasis During Training

A number of skills and attitudes deserve emphasis during training. They can be grouped into four areas:

1. group process skills
2. knowledge
3. resolving behavior problems
4. being compassionate, caring, helpful, and empathic without fostering dependence or rescuing

If a trainee experiences all three phases of training and is supervised, most of these areas will, as a matter of course, be covered in the training process. Still, the following list of special emphases can provide an evaluative tool for checking progress.

Group Process Skills

These skills include empathetic listening, tracking (ensuring that important areas of discussion that are interrupted or deviated from are eventually returned to), attaining an adequate balance between group maintenance needs and task accomplishment, and the difficult skill of being present to the group while simultaneously being aware of the group's process needs and progress towards the goals of the session. Finally, group process skills also include knowing when to deviate from session goals in order to attend to special needs or to branching opportunities that become available.

Knowledge

Although group leaders need to be knowledgeable with regard to chemical dependence and family systems, extensive knowledge for the beginner is not prerequisite. If both trainee and supervisor are honest and paying attention, any significant gaps in such knowledge will become obvious and can be attended to as the training proceeds. We particularly urge you to become increasingly familiar with the various support and mental health agencies, the self-help groups (including 12-Step programs), and the other community resources that are available to your children. Likewise, familiarize yourself with local special education referral processes. With such knowledge at your finger tips, you can refer a troubled child more quickly to the appropriate helping person or agency.

Resolving Behavior Problems

In the programs with which we are familiar, the support groups have been remarkably free of behavior problems. Adherence to group rules, which are repeated at the beginning of each session, and clarity about limits in a context that is clearly caring and non-judgmental go a long way in preventing most behavior problems. We have seen that invoking consequences such as "three strikes and you're out" (see page 36) is usually unnecessary, and rarely carried to the extreme of asking a child to leave the group. Our experience indicates that when behavior problems do occur, they are mainly of two kinds: the disruptive child who converses with someone else, interrupts, or acts out in some other way; and the child who puts others down. You can deal with behavior problems by clearly stating limits and rules and by exercising the most important skill of all to prevent troublesome difficulties: *communicating clearly and with an attitude of respect.*

Being Compassionate, Caring, Helpful, and Empathic Without Fostering Dependence or Rescuing

At times, acting in this manner can be very difficult. A fine line exists between being supportive in a therapeutic way and allowing dependent behavior that has the potential for slowing progress. On the one hand, a lot of children have lived lives deprived of adult love, affection, and support. Thus, as their caring and trusted group leader, you will quickly become an important person to them. On the other hand, if you allow a child to become too emotionally involved with you, his or her turmoil will only increase. That's why we say that you tread a fine line.

The issue here is mainly one of boundaries: It's appropriate for children to know that they can contact you in times of personal danger and confusion (for example, when confronted with personal abuse, fighting in the home, an unconscious parent); it's not appropriate for children to contact you just to chat. It's helpful and okay for you to explain to a child that you can be and want to be his or her friend; it's not helpful or all right to replace a parent or other primary caretaker in a child's life. You need to remind the children that they are ultimately responsible for taking care of themselves (although not by themselves) and that repeatedly being rescued will not serve them well.

Problems to Look Out For

In Chapter 6, we discussed a number of red flags or troublesome areas to watch for in selecting group leaders. You also need to keep a sharp eye out for these problematic areas of behavior after leadership training has begun. In fact, as mentioned in Chapter 6, some such problems may not even surface in an individual until he or she begins working with a group.

One of the most common problem behaviors is rescuing. Rescuing happens when a group leader encourages dependent behavior. The leader does this by repeatedly doing assigned tasks for a child, or by providing an inordinate amount of assistance with a task, or by giving verbal support that is devoid of attempts to persuade and assist a child to learn how he or she can help himself or herself. These rescuing behaviors reinforce the child's own dependent stance. For example, a third-grader constantly talks about how mom never listens. The facilitator who rescues repeatedly affirms the child's sadness and anger but never helps the child explore options such as "You're going to have to ask mom to listen—maybe ask her more than once, or find others who will listen."

Just as some parents try to live out their own frustrated needs and aspirations through their children by making an inappropriate emotional investment in their children's performance, so some group leaders may unconsciously play this same game by striving to derive self-worth from the progress the children make in group. Unfortunately, this behavior results in excessively encouraging or coercing a child to do something (join Little League, try out for the class play, or even draw another picture in group) long after the child has made the decision not to do so. Trying to derive self-worth from the progress children make in group is probably the most subtle form of unhealthy leadership. It's unhealthy for the leader and for the children.

Another, often subtle, difficulty is a leader's inability to show emotion—similar to the inability in a chemically dependent home. Since awareness and expression of feelings is one of the main goals of the support group program, a leader with difficulty in this area will obviously not set a good example. Like most issues, this one, too, has a flip side. Namely, it is possible for a leader to be too reactive emotionally. When this happens, your children will either feel acutely uncomfortable with you in group, or they will feel a need to take care of you. Again, this is an unhealthy situation for both the leader and the children.

Boundary issues can also become problematic. When we dealt with the section "Areas of Special Emphasis During Training" earlier in this chapter, we saw how issues concerning boundaries are crucial to healthy and successful group process. Here, we want to highlight boundary issues again and point out how they can be problematic in the areas of therapy and affection.

It is especially important that group leaders not use children's groups for their own therapy. A lot of spiritual growth and satisfaction, yes, but therapy, no. Self-disclosure can be used for the benefit of the group—always to help the children better understand their own lives—but be careful. *It's essential that group leaders get whatever support and therapy they need, but to get it elsewhere, not in the children's group.*

Boundaries are also important with respect to affection. We believe that therapeutic touch is part of the support and change process of young children. Hugs are fine, especially after being requested or initiated by the child, or after receiving the child's permission. Such initiative on the part of the child demonstrates an ability to take care of personal needs. Sitting in laps or within an embrace during a group session itself may be appropriate for a child who has been working through a particularly traumatic sharing or who has reported a particularly difficult time at home. As a general rule, however, such manifestations of affection are not good ideas. A well-meaning non-abusive facilitator may be using such demonstrations of affection to get his or her own needs met by the children in the group.

Likewise, be aware of favoritism. Some children need more attention than others during group sessions. On a given day, one child's needs and presentation may be so endearing that ignoring him or her is impossible. And that's okay. However, when the same child repeatedly gets the majority of your attention, the situation becomes troublesome. Other children quickly become aware of your "favorite." There is a key to avoiding favoritism: Give extra attention to those children who really need it, not simply to those whom you find it easier to deal with or like more than the others.

Finally, look out for aversion to conflict or frustration. A certain amount of conflict and frustration is healthy in our lives. Learning to move through these areas in a centered, grounded way is part of recovery and one of the valuable dividends of improved living skills. As a facilitator, your job is to help children learn to do just that. So, if your group is experiencing some frustration or conflict, help the children recognize that both can be resolved or lived through, that both are normal and growth producing. When frustrations and conflicts occur in group, don't avoid or ignore them, point them out. In fact, you could even give them names like, "family frustrations" or "family fight." Then, be a good model for the children as you work to resolve the frustration or conflict in a healthy way. What you're doing here is helping the children learn how to react appropriately and come through an uncomfortable experience without serious emotional consequences.

Training people to facilitate support groups may seem a daunting task. Actually, however, training is part of the ongoing process of group work. Leading groups and training leaders go hand in hand. As your program gets started, you'll recognize that training is one of its most exciting and fulfilling aspects. And, as more and more people volunteer to help more and more children, both the groups and the training will improve.

Selecting Children for Group

8

G ive special attention to the task of selecting children to participate in group. Support groups are most successful when they're filled (six to ten children). Filling a *Living Skills* group is usually not a problem. The task of filling a *Concerned Persons* group, however, is usually more complex; rarely do children affected by a loved one's chemical dependence rush to join the program. Rather, these children have learned well the rules of a chemically dependent family: *Don't talk. Don't trust. Don't feel.* As a result, these children keep the family secret well hidden until and unless they receive opportunities for support and assistance. Our experience has shown that three strategies can prove especially effective for encouraging children to enter a *Concerned Persons* group:

- Build a Referral Network
- Develop Recruitment Strategies
- Establish Group Membership Rules

These strategies also prove worthwhile in selecting participants for *Living Skills* groups. We encourage you to employ them as you select children for group membership.

Building a Referral Network

The first step in identifying appropriate children is to build a referral network that includes school staff, the community at large (including parents), and the school's student body.

The School Staff

Through in-service training, school staff members learn to identify students who exhibit high-risk behavior in the classroom. By understanding how the support group program operates and the services it provides, staff can refer children appropriately. The staff often plays a critical role in identifying children who have been affected by family chemical dependence.

The Community

Your referral network can extend beyond the school to the larger community. Share information about the support group program with parents, professionals, and other concerned adults at regularly scheduled community forums. Many parents will jump at the chance to have their children learn healthy life skills. Therapists and social workers from treatment centers and mental health agencies will be able to refer some of their clients to your program. A community counselor may refer a student to a *Concerned Persons* group while the student's parent is in treatment for chemical dependence.

The Student Body

Another referral source is your school's student body itself. Self-referrals are likely to begin as soon as youngsters become aware of the program and its value. No one in a school spreads good news faster than a satisfied student. We know of one wise third-grader who held court on the playground and told friends that they weren't to blame for their parents' drinking and fighting. This young fellow's enthusiasm caused many children to inquire after, and eventually to become part of, the school's support group program.

Developing Recruitment Strategies

The second step in involving appropriate children in your support group program is getting some recruitment (some "P.R."—public relations and program promotion) going in your school. The easiest way to begin is to publicize the program with classroom presentations. If your school has offered an in-class prevention curriculum, have the support group program leader and group leaders draw on this experience as they outline the new program for the students. Be sure to emphasize how support groups will help the children develop healthy living skills and lessen their chances of developing chemical abuse problems.

To encourage students to participate in the program, draw on the creativity and the creative people in your school: Design posters to hang in hallways and classrooms. Create a song or jingle about the program that invites student participation. Develop skits, puppet shows, or "commercials" for the program that involve the children and present them at student assemblies. Promote the support group program as much—or more!—as your school promotes other activities, like sports. As a follow-up to in-school promotion, ask the principal to send home a letter with each student that outlines and encourages program participation and invites parents to an orientation meeting. (See Example 8.1: Sample Promotion Letter, on pages 82 and 83.) These strategies can quickly swell the numbers of children seeking to participate in *Living Skills* groups.

Sometimes, however, they're not enough to reach the children most in need. Remember, a primary symptom of chemical dependence is denial, so not many members of a chemically dependent family, especially the children, will make a referral to a *Concerned Persons* group. Likewise, even after the best in-service training, school staff members are often unable to identify children from chemically dependent families because such children "hide" with incredible skill. Also, even if students exhibit some of the signs of belonging to a chemically dependent family—poor school performance, withdrawal,

Example 8.1   Sample Promotion Letter

Dear Parents:

As part of our school's continuing commitment to reduce alcohol and other drug use among youth, I am pleased to announce that we will be offering the (NAME OF SCHOOL)'s support group program. This program is dedicated to reducing risk factors for alcohol and other drug use by equipping children with basic living skills. Our support groups focus on the following life skills:

- identifying, expressing, and taking responsibility for feelings
- learning accurate, age-appropriate information about alcohol, other drugs, and chemical dependence
- developing problem-solving skills
- feeling good about oneself

The support groups will meet weekly and are open to all students. Groups run from eight to ten weeks. Participation in our support group program is voluntary, and parental permission is required.

I am sure that you are aware what a devastating impact alcohol and other drug use can have on children. Happily, research shows that children who have healthy living skills are much less likely to become involved with alcohol and other drugs. Our support group program is geared to provide your child with those skills. I wholeheartedly endorse the support group program and strongly encourage the participation of all students.

To help you learn more about the program and our efforts, I have scheduled an orientation meeting to be held on (DATE, DAY, TIME, & PLACE) . Please make plans to attend.

Example 8.1   Sample Promotion Letter

In the meantime, if you have any other questions or concerns, please contact me or (NAME & NUMBER OF APPROPRIATE CONTACT PERSONNEL—Program Coordinator or School Counselor) . Know that I look forward to seeing you on (DATE OF ORIENTATION MEETING).

Thank you for the chance to work with your child.

Sincerely,

hostile behavior—those signs may be the result of causes other than chemical dependence. Therefore, even with staff, community, and student body all directly and indirectly identifying prospects, some children fall through the cracks, especially children from chemically dependent families. Helping these children requires additional strategies for *Concerned Persons* group recruitment.

One effective strategy is to offer a different sort of classroom presentation, one that describes the impact of chemical dependence on the family. Enhance the presentation by including a film (see Appendix B for examples) or by inviting an Alateen member to share his or her personal experiences of growing up in a chemically dependent family. Make sure every student in the school gets a chance to view the presentation. Afterward, invite children to tell a teacher if they are interested in joining a group.

Another strategy is to follow up a presentation like the one described above with a questionnaire. (See Example 8.2: Student Questionnaire, on pages 86 and 87). After the presentation, give each student a copy of the questionnaire to fill out, assuring them that all their answers will remain confidential. Explain that some students will be invited to join a support group, but that it will be up to them to decide whether or not they want to join. Review the students' completed questionnaires. Note those that contain numerous "yes" responses. Finally, interview those "frequent respondents" individually to assess and discuss each child's suitability and desire to participate in a support group.

For your school's youngest students, employ a third strategy. After they view a presentation describing the impact of chemical dependence on the family, invite them to think if someone in their family makes them feel sad, afraid, or hurt because the person uses alcohol or other drugs. Then, to help the children decide if they want to join a support group, invite them to complete a drawing exercise. Provide crayons or colored markers. Give each child a picture that shows a number of children in a small group setting. (For a sample picture, see Example 8.3: Drawing Exercise, on page 88.)

Tell the children that they all can color the picture. Explain that if *they* would like to take part in a group, they should *draw themselves* in the picture. Review the children's completed drawings. Note the children who have added themselves to the picture. Then, as in the previous strategy, interview those children individually to evaluate and discuss each child's suitability and desire to participate in a support group.

These recruitment strategies work well. So be prepared for youngsters wanting to join the support groups. Once you start offering guidance, hope, and help, make sure your school has the resources necessary to serve an ever-increasing number of children.

Establishing Group Membership Rules

The third step in involving children in your support group program is setting sound guidelines for group membership. Doing so not only allows you to place children in the type of group that will best serve their needs, but also helps the entire program to run smoothly.

While any student may participate in a *Living Skills* group, it wouldn't be appropriate for a child to join a *Concerned Persons* group unless he or she—like everyone else in the group—had a family member harmfully involved with alcohol or other drugs. A youngster lacking this prerequisite wouldn't fit in, and were he or she present, the group's effectiveness might suffer. Many youngsters start out in a *Living Skills* group, identify a family member having a problem with alcohol or other drugs, and subsequently join a *Concerned Persons* group, which better fits their needs.

Three basic rules, which apply to both *Living Skills* and *Concerned Persons* groups, protect the individual, the group, and the integrity of the program.

Rule 1

Students most in need have the first chance to participate. Since the demand to participate often far outweighs openings in groups, prioritizing is the only equitable solution. If a student filled out a question-

Example 8.2   Student Questionnaire

Name _____ Date _____

Grade _____ Teacher _____

Answer the questions by circling yes or no. Take your time and answer all the questions. This is not a test. No one else will see your answers without your permission.

1. Are you worried about a family member's (parent, brother, sister, grandparent, or other relative) using alcohol or other drugs?   yes   no

2. Do you ever feel alone, scared, angry, hurt, or sad because a family member wasn't able to stop drinking alcohol or using other drugs?   yes   no

3. Do you ever think about hiding or emptying that person's bottles of alcohol or other drugs?   yes   no

4. Do you ever think that it's your fault that the person uses alcohol or other drugs too much?   yes   no

5. Do you ever wish that the person would stop using alcohol or other drugs?   yes   no

6. Do you ever feel afraid of upsetting this person because it might cause him or her to use alcohol or other drugs?   yes   no

Example 8.2   Student Questionnaire

7. Are you ever afraid or embarrassed to bring friends home because of a family member's using alcohol or other drugs?   yes   no

8. Do you ever feel afraid that the person in your family who uses alcohol or other drugs might hurt you, either on purpose or by accident?   yes   no

9. Do you ever feel that no one at home loves and cares about you?   yes   no

10. Would you like to talk to someone about a family member's using alcohol or other drugs?   yes   no

Note: In order for the children to respond appropriately and completely—especially children under the age of ten—it may be necessary to read the questionnaire aloud to them.

Example 8.3   Drawing Exercise

Name _____

naire (see pages 86 and 87), use that, as well as information gained in your interview with the student, to compare to information garnered from other students, and then to determine which students are most in need. For example, a third-grader whose parent was recently hospitalized probably has a greater need for a support group than a third-grader whose family hasn't had to deal with that circumstance.

Rule 2

Group welfare is more important than the potential needs of the individual. The group must always come first. Not all students' needs are best served by a support group. Occasionally a child's behavior in group may be so disruptive that the leader will have no choice but to remove the youngster from the group. Although this child has needs, it would seem that group cannot meet them. To help the child get his or her needs met, refer him or her to the school counselor, to a therapist in the community, or to the special education staff. Allowing the child to remain and interrupt and disrupt the group process is a grave disservice to the group, the leaders, and to the child.

Rule 3

Students have the choice to participate in support groups. You should never force a child into the program if he or she would rather not become involved.

Be aware that applying Rule 1 (students most in need have the first chance to participate) often can be difficult. For example, the family member whose chemical dependence is affecting a child may be his or her parent, sibling, grandparent, or other relative. Know, then, that generally the closer the child is to the dependent person, the more adversely affected the child will be.

Realizing this, however, you still have to recognize that every case is different and that there will always be exceptions to the rule. For example, a child may have a chemically dependent mother, but he or she may not have been in contact with the mother for years.

89

Another child may have a chemically dependent uncle—a seemingly "distant" relative—but live with that uncle every summer. Or a child may be concerned about doing or saying the wrong thing about a sibling who's returning home from an in-patient treatment program. Question children individually to resolve dilemmas like these. Explore problems, needs, and feelings related to the chemically dependent people in the children's lives. Finally, invite the children to join a support group, but be sure that they understand that it's their choice.

Leading Support Groups **9**

This chapter provides a week-by-week format for *Living Skills* and *Concerned Persons* support groups with specific instructions for facilitating each session. By understanding the program goals and how one session leads to the next, support group leaders can effectively teach key concepts and use activities and games to help reinforce those concepts.

Before You Begin

Before detailing the two formats of support groups, we offer you some helpful hints, relevant to both types of groups, to help you facilitate and lead a group more successfully.

1. A successful session hinges on thorough lesson planning done well in advance. Keep a notebook for lesson planning. Plan each meeting on a separate page. List the key concepts you wish to teach and the activities you plan to use to convey those concepts. If you wish, copy the lesson plan on an index card and keep it handy to refer to during the session. (See Example 9.1: Sample Lesson Plan, on page 92.) After a few weeks of group, you'll know fairly accurately the needs of your group members and what kind of activities work best for them.

Example 9.1   Sample Lesson Plan

Session 2 *Living Skills Group* *(4th–6th Graders)*
Understanding Feelings

Key Concepts:
1. All Feelings Are Okay
2. Talk About Feelings

Activities:
1. Brainstorm Feelings
2. Guess My Feeling Game
3. Drawing (optional)

Warm Up
Favorite Animal

Closer
Group Hand Squeeze

---

2. To help you deal with the wide developmental span of youngsters in elementary school, the overview in this chapter provides a couple of key concepts for each group session. After reading and discussing this material with your staff, choose the concept(s) you deem most appropriate for your particular group of children. Err on the side of simplicity; trying to present too much results only in confusion. Focusing on one key concept per session—or, perhaps, on two key concepts for older students—suffices.

3. Choose the key concepts to be presented in each session and, based on them, decide which activities will bring the concepts to life. Much of our work with elementary children is predicated on an old Chinese proverb:

When I hear, I forget.

When I see, I remember.

When I do, I understand.

Good activities not only get children up and moving, they also elucidate a key concept through an experience. Although we suggest and describe many activities below, we also urge you to try activities of your own, especially as you become more comfortable with leading groups. Let your own creativity blossom by developing new and exciting ways to help students learn. If you need more help, know that many good books provide activities for teaching living skills applicable to children. You'll find a number of such books listed in Appendix A.

4. Make sure the activities you choose are rich and varied. Include art, film, discussion, worksheets, and movement. You already know that children learn in a variety of ways—visually, auditorily, kinesthetically. Activities and games that incorporate these various learning styles allow you to reach more students more effectively.

5. Don't be afraid to get "in" where your students are "at." If children sit together on the floor, sit with them. If they sit in a circle of chairs, be part of the circle. Sit across from your co-leader to observe the group's dynamics and to facilitate better communication.

6. Make sure your lesson plans "fit the time." The sessions outlined in this chapter are designed to be completed in under an hour. If your school schedule allows only 30 to 45 minutes for a session, adjust your lesson plans accordingly. Always maintain a steady pace, one that neither bores nor overwhelms children.

7. Have fun. Allow the children to be children—to learn and to have fun at the same time. Participate in all the activities you ask the children to do. This helps them feel that all the activities are valuable for *everyone* and that you won't ask them to do anything you wouldn't do yourself.

Openers and Closers

As you plan each session, be sure to allow for both an opening time—*Opener*—to welcome the children and a closing time—*Closer*—to prepare them adequately for re-entry into their normal routine and to bid them farewell.

Openers

Many children are initially reluctant to share thoughts and feelings; some may remain reluctant throughout the entire group experience. Effective openers can counteract this. For elementary children, the opener (never lasting more than 5 minutes) can be something as simple as an open-ended question like "Who's your favorite cartoon character?" or "If you were king or queen of the world for one day, what one thing would you change?" Although youngsters always have the right to pass, responding to questions like these is fun. Openers make children more apt to become involved in the session from the outset. This is very helpful, for the longer children wait to speak up, the harder it becomes to do so. Openers also work to welcome children to group and to help them settle into the group's process. For a list of effective openers, see Example 9.2: Group Openers, on page 95.

Example 9.2   Group Openers

- Who is your favorite cartoon character?
- What food would you like to be on a hot day?
- If you were king or queen of the world for a day, what one thing would you change?
- What kind of animal do you feel like today?
- What is one special thing about your best friend?
- What is the best present you've ever gotten?
- If you could go anywhere on vacation, where would you go? Why?
- Where is a safe place you can go?
- What famous person would you like to meet?
- What is your favorite dessert?
- If you were stuck on a desert island, and only one person or thing could be brought to you, who or what would it be?
- What kind of food do you not like to eat?
- If you could have two wishes, what would they be?
- What is a feeling you have trouble talking about?
- What is something special about you?
- What would you like to be doing twenty years from now?
- What's something that really makes you laugh?
- What's your favorite day of the year?
- What's something you'd like to know more about?
- If you could be famous, what would you be famous for?

Closers

Always save the last 5 minutes or so of a session for closure. Group closers psychologically prepare children to go back to their usual environment. At the end of intense sessions, closers also provide a bit of calm to help children return to class, home, or other activities. Singing a favorite song, holding hands for a "group squeeze", having children tell about something nice they will do for themselves during the week are all good closers. Closers help children remember their special and unique qualities, prepare them for facing future challenges, and provide an opportunity for leaders to stress the group's common bond. For a list of effective closers, see Example 9.3: Group Closers, on page 97.

Overview of Living Skills and Concerned Persons Group Formats

Chapter 3 described the close similarities in the *Living Skills* and *Concerned Persons* groups. The chart on pages 98 and 99 depicts each group format in broad overview.

Example 9.3   Group Closers

---

1. The Serenity Prayer

Grant me the serenity to accept the things I cannot change, the courage to change the things I can, and the wisdom to know the difference.

2. Group Hug

Members stand in a circle with arms on the shoulders of the persons on each side. Everyone gives a squeeze hug.

3. Hand Squeeze

Members stand in a circle holding hands with one another. One member begins by squeezing the hand of the person on his or her right. The squeeze then continues around the circle of children.

4. Group "Highs"

Members share a highlight of their week since the last group session.

5. Wish List

Members share one thing they'll do over the coming week to take good care of themselves.

6. Joke Time

Volunteers share a favorite joke or two.

7. Song

Play or sing a song selected by the children as their group song:

We Are the World

The Greatest Love of All

You've Got a Friend

Living Skills Group

Session 1
Hellos and Welcome
Goals
• develop group rapport
• explain group rules and consequences

Session 2
Understanding Feelings
Goals
• create awareness of personal feelings
• facilitate communication skills

Session 3
The Great Feelings Cover-up
Goal
• develop insight into personal defenses

Session 4
Alcohol, Other Drugs, and Chemical Dependence
Goal
• present concepts on chemical dependence

Session 5
Our Special Families
Goal
• present basic concepts of the family system

Concerned Persons Group

Session 1
Hellos and Welcome
Goals
• develop group rapport
• stress the common bond (family member with chemical dependence)
• explain group rules and consequences

Session 2
Understanding Feelings
Goals
• create awareness of personal feelings
• facilitate communication skills
• explore the impact of family dependence

Session 3
The Great Feelings Cover-up
Goals
• develop insight into personal defenses
• create awareness of those situations to raise or lower defenses

Sessions 4 & 5
Alcohol, Other Drugs, and Chemical Dependence
Goals
• present concepts on chemical dependence
• stress how chemical dependence is not the children's fault
• discuss the chemically dependent family

Living Skills Group

Session 6
Taking Care of Me
Goals
• present problem-solving strategies
• increase awareness of community resources

Session 7
Celebrating Ourselves
Goal
• promote increased self-esteem and self-worth

Session 8
Good-byes and Hellos
Goals
• promote increased self-esteem and self-worth
• provide for group closure

Concerned Persons Group

Session 6
Our Special Families
Goals
• present basic concepts of the family system
• discuss how the family is affected by chemical dependence

Sessions 7 & 8
Taking Care of Me
Goals
• present problem-solving strategies
• increase awareness of community resources
• introduce a variety of self-care strategies

Session 9
Celebrating Ourselves
Goals
• promote increased self-esteem and self-worth
• give youngsters permission to celebrate their specialness

Session 10
Good-byes and Hellos
Goals
• promote increased self-esteem and self-worth
• give youngsters permission to celebrate their specialness
• provide for group closure

In-depth Exploration of Group Formats

To help you learn what you'll need to know and do throughout the program, let's take a session-by-session look at the two group formats. For each session, we will first present the concepts and activities for a *Living Skills* group—most of which are relevant and appropriate for a *Concerned Persons* group as well—and then we will present additional materials specifically geared for a *Concerned Persons* group.

Session 1 *Living Skills Group*

Hellos and Welcome

Key Concepts:

1. I can have fun in a group.
2. Group rules make it a safe place for me.

Suggested Activities:

1. *The Name Tag Grab Bag*
2. *Share Square*

Most elementary school children have probably never participated in a group process before. At the first group session, many of the children will be nervous, scared, and perhaps embarrassed. They'll have no idea of what to expect or how to behave. Therefore, after welcoming everyone, immediately explain the purpose of the group and state the group rules and consequences (see pages 34-37 for examples), explaining that their purpose is to ensure the children's safety. Remember to review group rules and consequences at the beginning of each session hereafter.

Devote the first session of a *Living Skills* group to helping the children get to know and feel more comfortable with one another. To put the children at ease, have some fun while you're getting acquainted. *The Name Tag Grab Bag* lets children do both simultaneously and quickly. Give each group member a blank name tag.

Have colored markers available. Ask the children to write their first name and to add decorations to one side of the tag. Display a number of differently decorated tags to get the children started. When everyone is finished, ask the children to think of something special about themselves—something they like to do, a hobby, a favorite place or game they enjoy—and to write it on the other side of the tag. Some children may need assistance, so circulate and offer help to any child who may need it. When the children finish writing, collect the tags and place them in a paper bag. Shake the bag and take out one tag, making sure to hide the name on the tag. Read aloud the "special something" on the tag and invite participants to guess whose tag it is. Repeat for all the tags and children. This icebreaker activity provides introductions, puts children at ease, and also stimulates smiles and laughter.

This session's second activity, *Share Square,* also helps everyone meet one another and learn more about one another. Have the youngsters sit to form a square. Direct the children to snap their fingers or clap their hands softly and rhythmically. Call out a question such as, "What's your favorite color?" Direct the children to answer one at a time, in order, around the square—"Blue," "Yellow," "Red," "Green," and so on—while the group continues the snapping or clapping. As soon as everybody's responded, ask another question— "What's your favorite food, game, TV show, time of year, day of the week, or animal?" or "What famous person would you like to meet?" or "What would you wish for from a fairy godmother?" Surprisingly, this activity reveals to the children their many similarities. To extend the Share Square game, encourage volunteers to ask other questions.

Session 1 *Concerned Persons Group*

Hellos and Welcome

Key Concepts:

1. I can have fun in a group.

2. Group rules make it a safe place for me.

3. I am not alone; others have chemical dependence problems in their families.

Suggested Activities:
1.   *The Name Tag Grab Bag*
2.   *Share Square*
3.   *Our Common Bond*

The activities used above in the first session of a *Living Skills* group also work very well in the first session of a *Concerned Persons* group. Know, however, that it is usually more difficult for children in a *Concerned Persons* group to feel at ease with one another. By the end of the first session, many of the children might be quite startled that, like themselves, everyone else in group lives with family chemical dependence. Many children don't realize that their condition is not an isolated one. If the *Share Square* activity goes well, make the following your last question for the exercise: "Who in your family has a problem with alcohol or other drugs?" The children's responses will help assess how they perceive the problem in their families.

We suggest adding an additional activity called *Our Common Bond* to the first session of a *Concerned Persons* group. Have the children sit on the floor in a circle. Holding a ball of yarn, remind the children that everyone in the group is concerned about a loved one's use of alcohol or other drugs. Ask the children to picture that person in their mind. Wrap a loose end of the yarn around one of your fingers, then roll the ball of yarn across the circle to one of the children. Ask him or her to wrap the yarn around a finger. Then invite the child to tell who in his or her family has the problem and, finally, to roll the ball of yarn to another child in the group. Before long, everyone in the group will be connected by the yarn, a tangible portrayal of their common bond—family chemical dependence. Note: if a child wishes to pass, allow this, but ask the child what he or she would like to get out of or to see happen in group.

Session 2 *Living Skills Group*

Understanding Feelings

Key Concepts:

1. All my feelings are okay.
2. There are people I can talk to about my feelings.

Suggested Activities:

1. Brainstorm feelings
2. *Guess My Feeling* game

Some youngsters live in family situations where feelings aren't acknowledged, let alone discussed. In order to cope, children in chemically dependent families learn not to feel. This session helps children identify, take responsibility for, and express their feelings.

After the session opener, have the children brainstorm feelings. List their ideas on a chalkboard or sheet of newsprint. To expose the children to a growing list of feelings, encourage them to identify as many as they can. Likewise, ask the children to describe the feelings as they are listed.

Note how some youngsters will come with only a handful of feeling words. Note, too, that words like "bad" or "mad" are not feeling words. If these words come up, point out that "bad" is a quality, not a feeling and that the feeling word for "mad" is "anger." This helps the children begin to identify real feelings. Thus, when a child says that he or she is feeling "bad," help him or her identify the real feeling that's behind that word, for example, "lonely," or "sad," or "afraid."

Draw from the children's list to lead a discussion of how feelings guide us through the day. Stress that all feelings are okay—that we all experience a wide array of them every day. Many children believe that some feelings such as anger, hurt, and fear are bad. Help the children understand that some feelings are just more uncomfortable

103

than others: "anger" might be more uncomfortable than "happy," or "hurt" can be more uncomfortable than "glad." Explain that it's what we do with our feelings that really counts. Emphasize that while all feelings are okay, it is never okay to hurt yourself or others when you have uncomfortable feelings.

Lead the group in the *Guess My Feeling* game, making sure that as many group members as possible have a chance to offer a feeling to be guessed. Begin the game by having a child come and whisper a feeling in your ear. The child then turns his or her back to the group. Direct the group to chant the chorus, "Turn, turn, turn in place, with a feeling on your face." As the group chants, the child slowly turns around, showing the feeling that he or she whispered to you, and the group members try to guess the feeling. Once correctly identified, ask the child to share a time he or she experienced that particular feeling.

Learning to own (take responsibility for) one's feelings is a fundamental life skill necessary for healthy communication with others. Children who can't own and express their feelings are at greater risk for a variety of problems, including alcohol and other drug use. So, instruct the group members to use "I" messages when sharing feelings and, as a group leader, model this behavior. For example, a child's saying, *"I feel angry when the kids make fun of me,"* reflects the child's ability to identify, take responsibility for, and express his or her feelings. Whenever you hear statements like these in group, be sure to validate them.

Session 2 *Concerned Persons Group*

Understanding Feelings

Key Concepts:

1. All my feelings are okay.
2. Some feelings are more uncomfortable than others.
3. There are people I can talk to about my feelings.

Suggested Activities:

1. Brainstorm feelings
2. Artwork-draw a picture of my family

Artwork can be a very useful additional tool to help a *Concerned Persons* group come to grips with feelings. Drawing allows children to express what they sometimes are unable to say. Provide the children with drawing paper, crayons, colored pencils, or markers. Either allow the youngsters to draw whatever they wish or give them instructions to draw something specific: their family, the dinner table, their parents. Circulate among the children as they draw, asking them about their drawings: how the people in the drawings might be feeling, how they feel as they draw. Encourage the children to use "I" messages in their responses to your questions. To maintain confidentiality, tell the children not to put their names on their work. Collect the drawings to be used for follow-up in the next group session. Note: Even if only one child draws a picture about family chemical dependence, know that everyone in group will be touched; members will see that they are not alone in their problems and that it's okay and safe to talk about them here.

Session 3 *Living Skills Group*
The Great Feelings Cover-up
Key Concepts:
1. Defenses are masks that hide my feelings from others and sometimes from myself.
2. I can learn about my own defenses.

Suggested Activities:
1. *Cover-up Game I*
2. *Cover-up Game II*

Defenses protect us from painful feelings. Youngsters from chemically dependent families may regularly utilize defenses to fend off painful emotions. Some youngsters, however, get stuck in their defenses, and they become a way of life. For example, some children defend themselves from painful feelings by constantly wearing an "everything's perfect" mask. They work very hard trying to be perfect: they're always smiling, have great grades, demonstrate leadership qualities, and offer assistance to others. They appear too good to be true. And, of course, they are. Under their facade of competency, these children are often troubled with powerful feelings of guilt and inadequacy—"If I can just do it (whatever "it" may be) right, things will get better at home."

Another common defense is clowning. Children who use this defense are always laughing, joking, teasing, and never seem to take anything seriously. Still other children use acting out behavior as a defense. They are rebels without a cause, always angry, and seeking negative attention. Behind their defensive mask lurks a very hurt and frightened child. Finally, some children simply defend themselves by withdrawing; they react only minimally to their surroundings and are quiet and isolated souls. The *Cover-up Game I* gives *Living Skills* group members a clear demonstration of defenses. Play this game as you would the *Guess My Feeling* game, except, just before the volunteer is about to turn and show his or her feeling face to the group, ask if you can cover his or her face with a cloth, sheet, or jacket (always ask permission). Then ask the other children to try and guess what feeling the volunteer is trying to show. It only takes a moment for the group to understand that the covering represents a defense that makes ascertaining the feeling impossible. Point out to the group that sometimes we cover our emotions, too, with defenses that prevent other people from knowing what we are really feeling.

After playing *Cover-up Game I,* go on to demonstrate some of the kinds of defenses we use by involving the children in *Cover-up Game II.* Before beginning the game, however, write the word "defenses" on the chalkboard or sheet of newsprint. Ask the youngsters to brainstorm defenses that they think could cover up feelings. Jot the group's ideas on the board or newsprint. If necessary, help the children discover at least the four defenses described above: behaving perfectly, clowning, acting out, withdrawing.

Prior to the session, draw four feeling faces—angry, happy, sad, scared—each on a separate piece of posterboard. After the brainstorming, show the group the drawings and call on different volunteers to describe the feelings pictured. Display the drawings in the meeting room. Give the children plain, white paper plates and drawing materials. Invite participants to draw pictures of masks that show defenses that could cover up any of the four feelings. When the children finish drawing, invite volunteers, one at a time, to hold their masks over one of the feeling faces. For instance, a child may draw a "clowning" mask and place it over the "sad" feeling face. Invite the child to describe his or her cover-up creation. Then, take the mask and tape it above the posterboard. Other children come up and repeat the process.

When all the masks are posted, draw attention to how people use lots of different defenses to hide their feelings. Point to different types of defense masks posted above the same feeling face, for example, a "clowning" mask and an "angry" mask posted above a "sad" feeling face. Explain to the children that once they become aware of their own defenses, they have choices about which ones they will use.

Conclude by helping the children discover how defenses can sometimes be a hindrance and sometimes a help. Ask:

- "Would a defense mask help if you were feeling sick and the school nurse wanted you to tell her where it hurt?" (No)
- "Would a defense mask help if a playground bully started picking on you and you felt afraid?" (Yes)

Session 3 *Concerned Persons Group*

The Great Feelings Cover-up

Key Concepts:

1. Defenses are masks that hide my feelings from others and sometimes from myself.
2. I can learn about my own defenses and when to raise and lower them.

Suggested Activities:

1. *Cover-up Game I*
2. *Cover-up Game II*
3. *Defenses Up, Defenses Down*

The same activities as used with a *Living Skills* group will help youngsters in a *Concerned Persons* group learn about defenses. In addition, try the following variation to *Cover-up Game II*. Instead of drawing four feeling faces yourself, use the children's drawings from their second session. Display the pictures in the room and encourage the children to describe any painful feelings they see illustrated.

Brainstorm defenses, as in the *Living Skills* group, making a list of defenses on the chalkboard or newsprint. Give the children plain, white paper plates. Explain that the plate is like a defense. It can cover up painful feelings. To demonstrate this, invite volunteers to cover one of the pictures that shows painful feelings with their plates. Then go on to provide the children with drawing materials and have them create defense masks, as in the *Living Skills* group, and continue the *Cover-up Game II,* having the children cover up their own "feeling" pictures with the masks they create.

Since many youngsters in a *Concerned Persons* group—children from chemically dependent families—have their defenses up much of the time, they very often cut themselves off from the support and guidance of healthy, caring adults or peers. To help the children see that they can raise or lower their defenses, lead the group in the *Defenses Up, Defenses Down* game.

Prior to class, devise a number of situations where children can decide whether to put up their defenses or to put them down. Write these scenarios on index cards. Present each scenario to the group. If the children think they should put their defenses up, have them indicate by giving a thumbs-up sign. If the children think they should put their defenses down, have them indicate by giving a thumbs-down sign. Here's an example of a situation: "A special volunteer asks you why you look so sad." The appropriate response would be "defenses down," because the counselor is a safe and trustworthy person. Another example: "Mom and Dad are fighting again." Here "defenses up" is appropriate, because it's not a good idea to get in the middle of parents fighting.

One final note about defenses. Although a certain defense might not be the healthiest way for a youngster to handle a particular problem, it may allow the child to survive his or her highly chaotic and unpredictable chemically dependent home. So never make a value judgment or attempt to take away any group member's defenses. Instead, empower the children by letting them know that they have the choice whether to raise or lower their defenses. *Defenses Up, Defenses Down* does a good job of helping youngsters practice this skill. Some children may eventually feel safe in letting go of a defense altogether, or they may be guided to use more socially acceptable defenses—withdrawing over lashing out. Although a child's certain defense may not always be appropriate, it also may not always be detrimental either to the child or to another person.

Conclude the session by explaining to the children that once they become aware of their own defenses, they can choose which ones to use, and they can choose whether or not to use them.

Session 4 *Living Skills Group*

Alcohol, Other Drugs, and Chemical Dependence

Key Concepts:

1. Alcohol and other drugs can change how people feel.
2. Some people use alcohol and other drugs as a defense to cover up painful feelings.
3. Children don't cause parents to become dependent on alcohol or other drugs.

Suggested Activities:

1. Film: *A Story About Feelings* or *Lots of Kids Like Us*
2. Group Discussion

Many children lack basic information about alcohol and other drugs and about the disease concept of chemical dependence. Showing one of these excellent films—*A Story About Feelings* and *Lots of Kids Like Us*—to your group can educate them in appealing and age-appropriate ways. *A Story about Feelings* not only details how alcohol and other drugs are too often used to cover painful feelings, but also shows the process of becoming dependent on these drugs. *Lots of Kids Like Us* portrays the experiences of two children living with parental alcoholism. To order either of these films, see Appendix B.

Spend the fourth session viewing and discussing one of the two films. Review and reinforce key concepts presented. Help the children understand that although not everyone who drinks alcohol or uses other drugs becomes dependent upon them, using either can be very dangerous. Especially point out the dangers for children using chemicals.

Sessions 4 & 5 *Concerned Persons Group*

Alcohol, Other Drugs, and Chemical Dependence

Key Concepts:

1. Alcohol and other drugs can change how people feel.
2. Some people use alcohol and other drugs as a defense to cover up painful feelings.
3. It's not my fault that family members are chemically dependent.
4. Chemical dependence runs in families, so I am at high risk.

Suggested Activities:

1. Film: *Twee, Fiddle, and Huff* (especially for grades K-3) or *Lots of Kids Like Us* (especially for grades 4-6)
2. Group Discussion
3. Film: *A Story About Feelings*
4. *Alphabet Soup*

For a *Concerned Persons* group, you will need to schedule two sessions (Sessions 4 and 5) to cover this crucial material. Even though chemical dependence is often the central unifying aspect of the lives of children in a *Concerned Persons* group, many lack accurate information about this disease. Most, for example, know and understand little about things such as blackouts, relapse, and recovery. The films *Twee, Fiddle, and Huff* (for younger children) and *Lots of Kids Like Us* (for older children) both delve into the experience of living in a chemically dependent family, provide valuable information, and can be springboards to rich group discussion. For information regarding ordering either film, see Appendix B.

Spend the fourth session viewing and discussing one of the two films. Review and reinforce key concepts presented in the film. Then call on volunteers to describe how their families are similar to the family in the film they saw. Stress that a parent's chemical dependence is not the children's fault. Make sure the children understand how important it is for them to learn to take care of themselves, and that by sharing in group they are learning how to do just that.

Begin Session 5 by showing another film, *A Story About Feelings.* This ten-minute film effectively reviews the previous session and refocuses the children's attention on the key concepts of the disease of chemical dependence. After viewing the film, give each group member a copy of an *Alphabet Soup*** sheet (see Example 9.4: *Alphabet Soup,* on page 114). Read aloud the 4 C's, one at a time, having the children repeat each after you. Allow the children time to discuss each C and how it applies to them. Proceed with the 5 S's, presenting each as above. Again, make sure the children have time to absorb and discuss each one. Give the children crayons, colored pencils, or colored markers and allow them to add decorations to their sheet. If time permits, have the children draw a picture on the opposite side of the sheet that shows them taking care of themselves.

Note: Throughout these two sessions, be sure to let the youngsters know that chemical dependence runs in families. Without preaching or frightening the children, explain that because chemical dependence runs in a family, they are at greater risk for such problems.

**From *Kids' Power: Healing Games for Children of Alcoholics* (Health Communications, 1989).

Example 9.4   Alphabet Soup

It's important for children from chemically dependent homes to remember the 4 C's and the 5 S's.

The 4 C's

1. I didn't **C**AUSE the chemical dependence.

2. I can't **C**ONTROL it.

3. I can't **C**URE it.

4. But I can learn how to **C**OPE with it.

The 5 S's

1. I didn't **S**TART the chemical dependence.

2. I can't **S**TOP it.

3. I don't have to **S**UFFER with it.

4. I don't have to feel **S**HAME because of it.

5. I can **S**AVE myself in spite of it.

Session 5 *Living Skills Group*
Our Special Families

Key Concepts
1. All kinds of families are special.
2. All families have good times, stress, and problems.

Suggested Activities:
1. *Favorite TV Families*
2. Group Discussion

According to the American Association of Marriage and Family Therapists, a child in America has a one-in-five chance of living through two divorces before reaching eighteen. Many youngsters today carry guilt and shame related to their families. This is even more likely and pronounced in high-stress family systems where workaholism, eating disorders, chemical dependence, and other problems exist. Even so, children consistently love and protect their families.

This fifth *Living Skills* session helps children celebrate their families—no matter their size, shape, or structure. As you lead the session, emphasize that every family has its good times, as well as its stresses and problems. Also, be clear that children don't cause parents to do things like separate or divorce. Too many children tend to shoulder the blame for these family problems.

Favorite TV Families is an activity that utilizes the knowledge children have acquired by watching television. Begin the activity by brainstorming the different kinds of TV families the children know. Write responses on the chalkboard or sheet of newsprint. As you list each family, list also its family structure: nuclear, two-parent, one-parent, two-partner, extended, adopted, racially mixed. Make sure the children recognize and understand the differences in family structures. Ask the children which TV family most represents their own.

Be sure to point out that all these families *are* families and that they are all special in their own way.

Have the group pick out one of the TV families with which most of them are familiar. Discuss the good times, stresses, and problems this TV family has (as portrayed on the TV show). Call on volunteers to share if their family has *ever* experienced any of these same good times, stresses, and problems. This lets the children see that all families experience these same phenomena.

Session 6 *Concerned Persons Group*
Our Special Families

Key Concepts:

1. All kinds of families are special.
2. Chemically dependent families have good times, stress, and problems.

Suggested Activities:

1. *Favorite TV Families*
2. Group Discussion
3. Family Collage

To lead a *Concerned Persons* group on the topic "Our Special Families," follow a similar procedure as for a *Living Skills* group. However, after listing the different TV families and their structures, ask group members to choose a particular TV family and describe what it would be like if someone in it were dependent on alcohol or other drugs. Many children will be quite open in discussing a fictional family. Since some of the group members may be living in recovering families, also discuss what the TV family might be like during recovery.

Invite the children to make family collages. Give each child a large sheet of construction paper or posterboard and a pair of scissors. Provide access to paste or glue sticks and old copies of magazines containing pictures that depict the various racial and cultural backgrounds of the children in group. Tell the children to look through the magazines and cut out any pictures they want and to make a collage that shows what their family is like. As the children work, spend time with each. Don't interrupt, but do allow the children to tell you about their collages. Afterward, have the children share in cleaning up. Then, if time permits, ask for volunteers to share masterpieces. Save the collages to post in the meeting room.

Session 6 *Living Skills Group*

Taking Care of Me

Key Concepts:

1. I can learn healthy ways to solve problems.
2. It's okay to ask for help.
3. There are people and places that can help me.

Suggested Activities:

1. Johnson Institute Problem-Solving Model
2. *Problem & Solution Game*

Many youngsters lack problem-solving strategies that are vitally important to them. This session not only helps children learn such strategies, but also assures them that asking for help in solving a difficult problem is okay and a sign of strength, not weakness.

Begin the session by asking volunteers to tell about a problem they recently had. Then, ask if they can tell how they solved the problem. You might hear about some simple problems that were solved by adults for the children, or some difficult problems that the children solved themselves after serious thought. Don't comment on any particular problem itself, but rather on the process the children used to solve it. For example, you might say, "It sounds like you worked very hard to solve your problem." Tell the children that in this session they will learn more about how to solve problems.

Distribute copies of the Johnson Institute Problem-Solving Model. (See Example 9.5: The Johnson Institute Problem-Solving Model, on page 120.) As you name and describe the six steps, write them on the chalkboard or sheet of newsprint. Enlist the children's ideas as you discuss each step. Take time to stress Step 5, "Locate resources for help." Tell the children that it is okay and smart to get help from others to solve problems. Likewise, let them know that it's also okay and smart to find a safe place to be when a problem is too difficult or dangerous.

Flesh out the model by having the children play the *Problem & Solution Game*. Prior to the session, outline three or four problems on index cards. For example:

For younger children:

> During recess, Tim was swinging on the playground swing. An older boy came up, grabbed the swing and told him to get off. Tim had waited his turn to swing and did not want to get off, but he was afraid of the older boy. What should Tim do?

For older children:

> Melissa and Emma were invited to Gena's house to play after school. Melissa said that she could come. But Emma's parents had a rule that she couldn't be at anyone's house if parents weren't home. Gena's parents were not going to come home until 6:30. What should Emma do?

Take the children through the steps, and ask for their help in identifying the possible choices and their consequences on the chalkboard or newsprint. Encourage the children to explore the widest possible range of legal and permissible choices. Again, pay particular attention to Step 5. You might want to list names of safe people, safe places, or make available a list of local resources for help. When it comes to Step 6, you might want to have the children—especially younger children—illustrate their solution to the problem.

Sessions 7 & 8 *Concerned Persons Group*
Taking Care of Me

Key Concepts:

1. It's okay to ask for help.
2. There are people and places that can help me.
3. It's important always to stay safe.

Example 9.5   The Johnson Institute Problem-Solving
Model

1. Name the problem. (What is it?)

2. Identify feelings. (How do I feel?)

3. Identify choices. (How can I solve the problem?)

4. Examine possible consequences. (What might happen if I choose this way or that way to solve the problem?)

5. Locate resources for help. (Where can I get help? Who can help me?)

6. Select the best possible choice. (Which choice helps me stay safe and lets me take care of myself?)

Suggested Activities:

(1) Johnson Institute Problem-Solving Model

(2) *Safe/Unsafe People*

(3) *Wheel of Misfortune*

For a *Concerned Persons* group, you will need to devote two sessions (Sessions 7 and 8) to empower group members with positive, healthy coping strategies. For the first such session (Session 7), follow the procedure for a *Living Skills* group (Session 6) as described above, with one variation. When fleshing out the Johnson Institute Problem-Solving Model, include at least one problem typical of a chemically dependent family. For example:

> Steve's mom promised to take him to the Zoo on Saturday morning. On Friday night, Steve's mom went to a party where alcohol was served. On Saturday morning, when Steve went into his mom's room to wake her up, she got angry, said she felt sick, and told Steve to go away and be quiet. What should Steve do?

Prior to the second session on this topic (Session 8), list the six steps of the Johnson Institute Problem-Solving Model on the chalkboard or newsprint. If you wish, and if the children don't have their own copies of the steps, which you gave them in Session 7, have additional copies available. Begin Session 8 with a thorough review of the model. Then introduce *Wheel of Misfortune*, a problem-solving game that emphasizes staying safe and self-care strategies.** (See Example 9.6: Wheel of Misfortune Gameboard, on page 122.)

**From *Kids' Power: Healing Games for Children of Alcoholics* (Health Communications, 1989).

Example 9.6   Wheel of Misfortune Gameboard

Prior to the session, get ten index cards. Print a letter ("A" through "J") on each individual card and place the cards in a lunch bag. The letters correspond to one of the problem situations outlined in Example 9.6. Divide the children into two groups. Give each group a copy of the Wheel of Misfortune Gameboard (Example 9.6). Note: You may also outline this on the chalkboard or newsprint. Tell the small groups to draw a card from the bag and to work together to solve the problem on the gameboard that corresponds to the letter on their card. Encourage the children to follow all six steps of the Johnson Institute Problem-Solving Model as they work through their sample problems.

Working together, the children will begin to realize that they have choices and options in handling tough situations—this is empowering. As the children work, emphasize again the people and places in the community that can be a help to them. Children can never have too many helping resources.

Session 7 *Living Skills Group*

Celebrating Ourselves

Key Concepts:

1. Everyone has special qualities.
2. It's okay to feel good about myself.

Suggested Activities:

1. Group Discussion
2. Gift Bags
3. Song(s)

This session celebrates each youngster's special gifts. To affirm who the children are and to boost their self-esteem, the session helps children feel good about themselves, learn how to treat others well, and move closer to a peaceful acceptance of who they are.

To stress how everyone has special qualities or gifts and to define "special gifts," have the children identify the special gifts that exist in their group, such as Jimmy's creativity, Betsy's thoughtfulness, and Siobhan's listening skills. Make sure that each child has one of his or her special gifts mentioned. Stress that everyone has special gifts.

Have the children make "gift bags." Give youngsters lunch bags and decorating materials. Have children put their first names on the bags, then decorate the bag in any way they wish. When the children finish, line up the bags in the room. Provide access to a number of blank index cards. Tell the children to write—or draw an illustrative picture of—a special gift of each group member, each on a separate index card, and then to drop the card into the person's "gift bag." (Note: You may have to help younger children who have difficulty with printing, spelling, or reading.) Soon, everyone will have a bag filled with wonderful gifts.

Allow the children a few moments to read and explore their gift bags. Then let each child share one compliment from his or her bag.

Be sure that you compliment the children on their cooperation and caring. Point out that when they receive compliments, children can say "thank-you."

To end the session, sing a song that celebrates the children and that everyone in the group knows and likes.

Session 9 *Concerned Persons Group*

Celebrating Ourselves

Key Concepts:

1. Everyone has special qualities, even people who are chemically dependent.

2. It's okay to feel good about myself.

Suggested Activities:

1. Group Discussion

2. Gift Bags

3. Song(s)

To help children in a *Concerned Persons* group celebrate themselves, use the same strategies and activities provided for *Living Skills* groups. Many children from chemically dependent families have a lot of difficulty receiving compliments.

The only addition necessary to a *Concerned Persons* session is to help the children recognize that chemically dependent people also possess "special gifts," which, sadly, are hidden or partially obscured by their disease. If you wish, allow the children to talk about the special gifts possessed by their chemically dependent family member(s). The additional point to be made here is that while chemically dependent people have a terrible disease, they are not terrible people.

Session 8 *Living Skills Group*

Good-Byes and Hellos

Key Concepts:

1. It's okay to celebrate my special qualities.
2. I can say good-bye to group and hello to a new me.

Suggested Activities:

1. *Share Square*
2. Certificates/Evaluation
3. Party

This final session is devoted to closure and celebration. It provides you with an opportunity to acknowledge and affirm the new skills the children have acquired and the risks they've taken to try out those skills. Finally, in this session the children bid farewell to group and say hello to the new person they've become.

Begin the session with *Share Square* (see Session 1). Have the youngsters sit to form a square. Direct them to snap their fingers or clap their hands softly and rhythmically. Once everyone is together and in rhythm, you, as group leader, should say aloud, for each child in the group, one of his or her unique qualities. For example, "Chris, you show everyone respect" or "Alice, you are very patient." After you have complimented everyone in the group, invite the children to state aloud one of his or her own gifts. Once the children get this extra boost, invite anyone who wishes to express any final comments about group. Be sure to thank all the children for their participation.

Present certificates of completion or accomplishment to each child. (See Example 9.7: Certificate, on page 127.) As each child receives a certificate, encourage the group to offer applause and a congratulatory cheer. Afterward, ask everyone to fill out a group evaluation form. (See Example 9.8: Participant Evaluation, on pages

126

Example 9.7   Certificate

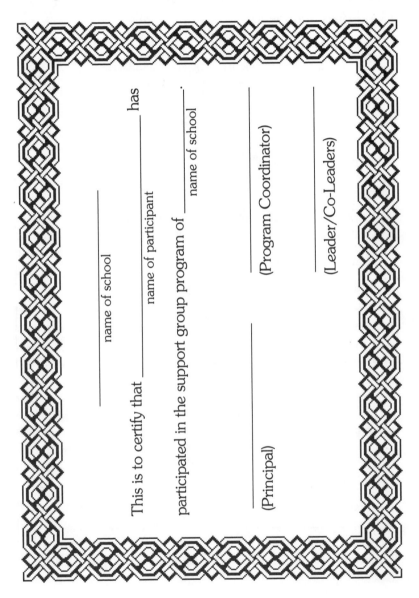

Example 9.8   Participant Evaluation***

Grade:_____ Group:_____

Date:_____

Write out your answers to the following.

The things I liked best about group:

1. _____

2. _____

3. _____

The things I didn't like about group:

1. _____

2. _____

3. _____

Some important things I learned in group:

1. _____

2. _____

3. _____

Games and activities that were the most fun:

1. _____

2. _____

3. _____

***It's advisable to ask these questions verbally of young children (K-2) and record their responses yourself.

Example 9.8   Participant Evaluation

Games and activities that were the least fun:

1. _____

2. _____

3. _____

Circle the best answer for you.

I think group helped me:	Lots	Some	A Little	Not at All
Talk about how I feel	Lots	Some	A Little	Not at All
Learn about alcohol and other drugs	Lots	Some	A Little	Not at All
Learn how to take care of me	Lots	Some	A Little	Not at All
Have fun	Lots	Some	A Little	Not at All
I think the group leaders helped me	Lots	Some	A Little	Not at All

---

128 and 129. See also Chapter 10, pages 135-140, for more on evaluations.) As the participants fill out the evaluation sheets, make final preparations to serve snacks and juice.

Conclude the session and the group with a party; share food and drink. If you wish, also provide recorded music or sing favorite songs. Be sure to bid each child a personal farewell and to send each away with an expression of your thanks and pride.

Session 10 *Concerned Persons Group*
Good-Byes and Hellos
Key Concepts:
1. It's okay to celebrate my special qualities.
2. I can say good-bye to group and hello to a new me.

Suggested Activities:
1. *Share Square/Telephone Game*
2. Certificates/Evaluation
3. Party

Lead a concluding *Concerned Persons* group session in the same way as you would a *Living Skills* group session. You may, however, add the *Telephone Game* activity to reinforce the major concepts shared in group. Have the children join you in forming a circle. Whisper an important message in the ear of the child next to you. Good examples of such messages are:

- "You're not alone."
- "It's not your fault."
- "Feelings are okay."
- "You can take good care of yourself."
- "Ask safe people to help you with problems."

Have the child repeat the message by whispering it in the ear of the child next to him or her and so on, until the message has traveled the entire group circle. Then share a new message.

If group members are willing, augment the game by allowing the children to exchange telephone numbers so that they can keep in touch with one another. Then, go on to present certificates, evaluate, and celebrate.

Note: Be aware that some children may find it difficult for group to close. So don't be surprised if some defenses go up or if behavior regresses a bit. Be ready to assure the children that they have come a long way and have learned a lot. Let each child know how proud you are of him or her.

Important Extra Program Tips

As you begin to lead support groups for elementary children, there are a couple of useful suggestions you ought to keep in mind. First of all, it is generally prudent not to allow children to take home any work they do in the support group—art, stories, collages, related items. This will ensure that none of the children's creations will risk becoming the focus for derision or anger, or be used against them in any other way. Should something like that occur, it would not only be counter-productive in and of itself, but would also cause the child to feel unsafe in the support group. The only exception to this rule would be something made in group that reflects a child's own special qualities or gifts, for example, the "gifts bags" in *Living Skills* Session 7 and *Concerned Persons* Session 9.

Second, we also suggest that after each group meeting, you have the children take home a note to their parents, written by the program coordinator or group leader, which outlines the session's theme and key concepts. (See Example 9.9: Updating Letter to Parents, on pages 132-33.) Each letter could also offer one or two ways parents or guardians could follow up on the learning that took place in the session. For example, the letter that goes home explaining Session 2, "Understanding Feelings," might suggest that parents

Example 9.9   Updating Letter to Parents

(Date)

Dear Parents,

The theme of our second group session was UNDERSTAND-
ING FEELINGS. Through brainstorming, games, and group discussion, group leaders helped your child understand that all of his
or her feelings are okay. Your child also discovered that some feelings are more discomforting to have and more difficult to express
than others. For example, anger is more uncomfortable to have
and more difficult to express appropriately than is happiness.
Together, the group discussed appropriate ways to deal with feelings. Finally, in the group leaders, your child found other "safe"
persons with whom he or she could share and discuss feelings.
You should know that throughout the group sessions, leaders will
continue to help your child learn how to recognize other "safe"
people in whom he or she can confide.

Learning how to identify and express feelings in safe and
appropriate ways is an invaluable living skill for your child. You
can support our group efforts by trying one of the following suggestions with your child this week:

1. Be alert for times when your child expresses—or wishes to
    express—feelings. When this happens, listen attentively with-
    out commenting on the feeling itself. This helps your child
    recognize that all his or her feelings are okay.

Example 9.9   Updating Letter to Parents

2. At bedtime, have your child share two feelings that he or she experienced during the day—one comfortable feeling and one uncomfortable feeling. Then reciprocate and share a couple of your feelings with your child. This simple activity will help you and your child feel more comfortable about sharing feelings with one another.

3. Make sure that your child understands who the "safe" people are in his or her life. Safe people could be parents, grandparents, siblings, other relatives, a trusted neighbor, a teacher, or a clergyperson.

Thank you so much for the gift of working with your child. Like you, we recognize that your child is special, talented, wonder-filled, and quite precious. We promise to continue to take good care.

Sincerely,

(Co-leaders)

be alert for times when their child expresses—or wishes to express—feelings and, when this happens, to listen attentively without commenting on the feeling itself. Lastly, the letter should affirm and acknowledge the adults for allowing their children to participate in the support group program. Letters like these will help parents feel part of the program and will offer them some tools to help their children and themselves as well.

When Groups End, What Then? **10**

O nce the exhilaration of hugs, applause, cheers, and certificates has passed, important tasks remain for the group leaders. First of all, group leaders must discuss and evaluate the progress of each group member and recommend appropriate follow-up: participate in another group; refer to community services; refer to special education staff; no specific follow-up required at this time. Second, to improve the program, leaders must examine and evaluate group structure and function: how effectively the sessions met the children's needs; how the process may be improved; what games and activities might better help the youngsters understand key concepts; and how to improve themselves as group facilitators. This chapter addresses these issues.

Evaluating Group Members

During the last two group sessions, the leaders should tell group members that after group ends, they all will be seen individually for follow-up. Before meeting with the children, co-leaders should meet to discuss each youngster's progress and to agree on their recommended follow-up. Some recommendations are best given with the school counselor or other referral source involved in the discussion.

Some children make great strides in group. They openly and honestly express feelings and demonstrate a variety of healthy coping skills. They use group to test and deepen these skills. For such children, additional program involvement is usually not necessary once group has ended. Leaders simply acknowledge these children's steady strides and remind them that group is a valuable resource if they should experience problems later on.

For other children, group opens their eyes to new concepts and skills. While making good progress, some of these children need additional support. For example, while participating in a *Living Skills* group, a child may realize that a family member is chemically dependent. This child could benefit from a recommendation or referral to take part in a *Concerned Persons* group.

Although it is generally a good rule not to have children participate in the same kind of support group again, the *Concerned Persons* group is an exception. Youngsters, especially those living with active chemical dependence or the early stages of recovery, may benefit from taking part in a second cycle of *Concerned Persons* group sessions to help them reinforce and deepen their growing coping skills. Other children might still need continued support and involvement, which could be provided through participating in an "old-timers" group. This group could meet weekly, but it would not rely on weekly themes. Rather, it would simply afford participants the opportunity to share personal problems and concerns and to practice the living skills they already learned in their *Concerned Persons* group.

Leaders may also make referrals to community programs that provide services for children and families who are involved with chemical dependence problems. Another appropriate follow-up is referral to sports, Scouts, or other social clubs or organizations that give children opportunities to work and play with others.

Unfortunately, not all children are best served by school-based support groups. Some group members may exhibit psychological or behavioral problems that require more individual attention and help than the support group program or the school can offer. To meet the needs of these children effectively, leaders should refer them to community agencies, special education staff, or private therapists. Facilitators, in cooperation with school counselors, should not hesitate to refer children to such services if the support group program fails to meet their needs.

If a child was initially referred to the program, facilitators should contact the source of the referral before making any final recommendation. For example, if a fourth grade teacher referred a withdrawn student to your *Living Skills* group, inform the teacher that the child has completed the group, what progress has been made, and ask input for your follow-up recommendation. If a father originally referred his daughter to your *Concerned Persons* group, meet with the father and the school counselor. As a result of that meeting, you might suggest to the father that his daughter would be best served by a community counseling center that offers primary services to children from chemically dependent families. As a group leader, you need to work in cooperation with your school counseling office whenever a follow-up involves the outside community.

Group leaders need to remember that they are like farmers, planting seeds within every child. In some children, the seeds take root immediately and quickly yield an abundant harvest. There's nothing more exciting than to watch the confidence of a once uncertain, self-defeating sixth-grader rise swiftly as she comes to realize and accept her special gifts in a *Living Skills* group. Or, the second grade boy who admits that his mom is using cocaine, works through some tears, and comes to believe deep inside that it's not his fault. In other children, the seeds you plant will take longer to germinate and root, and their harvest is long in coming. Know, however, that children understand what they're able and ready to do at any particular time. Like the farmer, your job as a group leader is to plant the seeds, nurture them along, and, most of all, to wait patiently.

137

Evaluating Your Support Group Program

A successful and effective support group program evaluates its experience, structure, and process to improve its effectiveness in reaching children who need help. This involves evaluating group members, the group experience, and the facilitators.

We discussed evaluation of the group members in the previous section. Some children make obvious and rapid gains, while others may appear to have gained little or nothing from the experience. However, collective analysis of all the children's evaluations will provide you the most valuable data for evaluating the program's effects on them. Did the group meet the needs of its participants or not? That is the bottom line.

Assessment of the group experience needs to have input from the facilitators, from the youngsters (the experts in this arena), and sometimes from the parents as well. Although more elaborate questionnaires can be formulated to provide more data, the most important questions to be answered by facilitators are:

- Did this group cycle meet the program's stated goals and objectives?
- Did the children have an opportunity to play—to be children? If not, which sessions were the most/least fun?
- Were there concepts or experiences that group members had difficulty "getting"? What were they?
- Are there better ways we might have made such and such a point?
- Which activities and games produced the most response and energy from the children? Which produced the least?
- What worked well? What not so well? What worked poorly?
- Was there anything about attendance patterns that we need to pay attention to?

Group leaders may ask the children similar questions, worded appropriately, either verbally or in a simple, evaluative questionnaire (see Example 9.8: Participant Evaluation, on pages 128-29).

We emphasize again the importance of getting participant input. By asking children about their experience in group, facilitators can glean invaluable answers to questions like those above and to others as well. Once you've obtained the children's responses, co-leaders must allow themselves time to discuss them and to add their own impressions. You can then examine and consider this combined data at a meeting of all the program's facilitators and other personnel.

Finally, an evaluation of facilitators' skills is also an essential part of program evaluation. Assess leaders' strengths and liabilities from a variety of sources, including, but not limited to, questions regarding leaders on the participants' evaluation forms and the regular debriefings where leaders honestly pinpoint one another's strong and weak points. In addition, the facilitators' meeting offers a safe place both to assess one's abilities and to receive the suggestions and critique of one's peers. Such meetings—which we suggest be held twice a month—allow everyone connected with the program to come together for support, skill building, and the opportunity to share problems, concerns, and success stories. If at all possible, arrange for an outside consultant to meet with the program staff at least once a year for additional training and for staff replenishment.

Based on these kinds of evaluative input, the program can be modified and adapted to best meet participants' needs. For instance, if activities in *Living Skills* groups took on an increasingly serious tone, feedback from both children and leaders would hopefully indicate a need to make these groups a bit more fun. Likewise, if leaders determine that children in the *Concerned Persons* groups failed to understand problem-solving strategies, leaders may decide that more time is needed to convey and practice these important strategies and skills.

Evaluating the program allows its structure to grow in a rich, dynamic way and provides suggestions for group leaders to modify their approaches to the benefit of the children. All group leaders can improve. That's why it's important for them to explore their strengths while working to enhance them. There are many resources to help—formalized support group leader training; course work on chemical dependence and co-dependence; and seminars on sensitivity to the cultural diversity of group members. Attending Al-Anon meetings can also help group leaders detach from taking on all their group members' problems and concerns. Finally, since it is so important for leaders to give themselves permission to enjoy the group experience, we suggest that they occasionally take a break from leading groups. Group leaders need time off, too—for their own good and for the good of the entire support group program.

Conclusion

We believe that support groups can profoundly change the lives of elementary school children. We are certain that offering K-6 children a support group program like the one outlined in this book gives them the opportunity to acquire the skills and motivation they will need to preserve and increase their health and ways of healthful living throughout their lives. We know that support groups work and work well. And we urge you to experience this for yourself.

It's true that it takes many steps and considerable work to set up a support group program in an elementary school. But the hardest step is the first, and it takes only one or two educators with a vision for change to take this step. You can take it, and you'll have help on the way. A variety of sources can offer you the support of group facilitator training. Various books and films on small group structure, chemical dependence, and leadership skills, and, of course, the material contained in this book can be your guides. So, proceed slowly, modifying format and style to best fit the needs of your students and school, but proceed.

Once you set out, the momentum will build. Yes, there will be more to do: groups to be offered, leaders to be trained, networks to be established, more children to be reached and served. Meanwhile, your program will have become its own best testimonial; it will give children a safe place to talk about feelings and to learn a variety of life skills; it will allow children to be children—to laugh and play; and it will celebrate its own success through the openness and vitality of all who participate and change.

As you and the program progress, be sure to have fun yourself. When confronted with obstacles, remember to focus on the difference you have made in the children's lives: Jimmy's once-pocketed hands now reach out for help; LaShunda is now finding healthy ways to deal with her family's chemical dependence problem; Jose's indifference is being transformed into a shy willingness; Marissa is concentrating on her schoolwork; and most of the children are communicating better with their parents. Providing youngsters with opportunities like these is an incredibly significant accomplishment and its own reward. Delight in that.

As more and more children and teachers become involved in the effort to improve and enhance their own health and well-being, we are convinced that their collective power will speak loudly to those around them. As individuals progress on their way to healthy, drug-free living, the world of sound and sober people will expand. In that world, love, peace, and self-assured assertiveness will replace hate, turmoil, and anger (the confederates of dependence and co-dependence). That is the world that all of us want. That is the world that our children deserve.

Appendix A:
Books and Pamphlets

Ackerman, R.J. *Children of Alcoholics: A Bibliography and Resource Guide*. Pompano Beach, FL: Health Communications.

Ackerman, R.J. *Children of Alcoholics: A Guidebook for Educators, Therapists, and Parents*. Holmes Beach, FL: Learning Publications.

Al-Anon Family Group Headquarters. *What's Drunk, Mama?* New York: Al-Anon Family Group Headquarters.

Anderson, Gary L. *Enabling in the School Setting*. Minneapolis: Johnson Institute.

Anderson, Gary L. *When Chemicals Come to School: The Student Assistance Program Model*. Minneapolis: Johnson Institute.

Anderson, Gary L. *Solving Alcohol/Drug Problems in Your School*. Minneapolis: Johnson Institute.

Black, Claudia. *My Dad Loves Me—My Dad Has a Disease*. Newport Beach, CA: ACT.

Brooks, Cathleen. *The Secret Everyone Knows*. San Diego: Operation Cork.

Cermak, Timmen L., M.D. *Diagnosing and Treating Co-dependence: A Guide for Professionals Who Work with Chemical Dependents, Their Spouses, and Children.* Minneapolis: Johnson Institute.

Clark, K.K. *Grow Deep Not Just Tall.* St. Paul, MN: CEP.

Clarke, Jean I. *Self-Esteem: A Family Affair.* Minneapolis: Winston Press.

Figueroa, Ron. *Pablito's Secret.* Pompano Beach, FL: Health Communications.

Fluegelman, A. (ed.) *The New Games Book.* Garden City, NY: Dolphin Books.

Goldberg, L. *Counseling for Children of Alcoholics.* Tallahassee, FL: Apalachee Community Mental Health Services.

Hastings, J. and Typpo, M. *An Elephant in the Living Room.* Minneapolis: Comp Care Communications.

Hornick, E. *You and Your Alcoholic Parent.* New York: Associated Press.

Jones, P. *The Brown Bottle.* Center City, MN: Hazelden.

Leite, Evelyn. *Detachment: The Art of Letting Go While Living with an Alcoholic.* Minneapolis: Johnson Institute.

Lerner, R. and Naiditch, B. *Children Are People Support Group Training Manual.* St. Paul, MN: Children Are People.

Melquist, E. *Pepper.* New York: National Council of Alcoholism.

Moe, Jerry. *Voices from the Heart: Recovery for Kids.* Redwood City, CA: The Children's Place.

Moe, Jerry, and Pohlman, Don. *Kid's Power: Healing Games for Children of Alcoholics.* Pompano Beach, FL: Health Communications.

Morehouse, E., and Scola, C. *Children of Alcoholics: Meeting the Needs of the Young CoAs in the School Setting.* South Laguna, CA: National Association for Children of Alcoholics.

National Association for Children of Alcoholics. *It's Elementary: Meeting the Needs of High-Risk Youth in the School Setting.* South Laguna, CA: National Association for Children of Alcoholics.

Seixas, J. *Alcohol: What It Is, What It Does.* New York: Greenwillow Books.

Seixas, J. *Living with a Parent Who Drinks Too Much.* New York: Greenwillow Books.

Ways, Peter. *Kids' Kamp: A Healing Experience for Children.* Redwood City, CA: The Children's Place.

Wegscheider-Cruse, S. *Another Chance.* Palo Alto, CA: Science and Behavior Books.

Wilmes, David. *Parenting for Prevention: How to Raise a Child to Say No to Alcohol/Drugs—For Parents, Teachers, and Other Concerned Adults.* Minneapolis: Johnson Institute.

Appendix B: Films

A Story About Feelings, Johnson Institute, 7151 Metro Boulevard, Minneapolis, MN 55439-2122.

All Bottled Up, AIMS Media Inc., 626 Hustin Avenue, Glendale, CA 91201.

Lots of Kids Like Us, Gerald T. Rogers Productions, 5225 Old Orchard Road, Suite 23A, Skokie, IL 60077.

Poor Jennifer, She's Always Losing Her Hat, National Association for Children of Alcoholics, 31582 Coast Highway, Suite B, South Laguna, CA, 92677-3044.

She Drinks a Little, Learning Corporation of America, 1350 Avenue of the Americas, New York, NY 10019.

Soft Is the Heart of a Child, Operation Cork, 8939 Villa La Jolla Drive, San Diego, CA 92037.

Twee, Fiddle, and Huff, Johnson Institute, 7151 Metro Boulevard, Minneapolis, MN 55439-2122.

Where's Shelly? Johnson Institute, 7151 Metro Boulevard, Minneapolis, MN 55439-2122.

To order films available from the Johnson Institute, call
TOLL-FREE:

1-800-231-5165

In Minnesota call:
1-800-247-0484
or **(612) 944-0511**

In Canada call:
1-800-447-6660

Appendix C:
National Resources

The following resources can provide excellent additional information on preventing alcohol and other drug use by children.

A. A.
Alcoholics Anonymous
General Service Office
P. O. Box 459
Grand Central Station
New York, NY 10163
(212) 686-1100

Addiction Research Foundation
33 Russell Street
Toronto, Ontario M5S 2S1
CANADA
(416) 595-6056

Al-Anon Family Group Headquarters
1372 Broadway
New York, NY 10018-0862
(212) 302-7240

Alateen
1372 Broadway
New York, NY 10018-0862
(212) 302-7240

American Council for Drug Education
204 Monroe Street
Rockville, MD 20850
(301) 294-0600

COAF
Children of Alcoholics Foundation, Inc.
200 Park Avenue, 31st Floor
New York, NY 10166
(212) 351-2680

Families Anonymous
World Service Office
P. O. Box 528
Van Nuys, CA 91408
(818) 989-7841

Families in Action Drug Information Center
2296 Henerson Mill Road
Suite 204
Atlanta, GA 30345
(404) 325-5799

Hazelden Foundation
Box 11
Center City, MN 55012
(800) 328-3330

IBCA
Institute on Black Chemical Abuse
2614 Nicollet Avenue South
Minneapolis, MN 55408
(612) 871-7878

Johnson Institute
7151 Metro Boulevard, Suite 250
Minneapolis, MN 55439-2122
(800) 231-5165

NACoA
National Association for Children of Alcoholics, Inc.
31582 Coast Highway, Suite B
South Laguna, CA 92677-3044
(714) 499-3889

Narcotics Anonymous
World Services Office, Inc.
P. O. Box 9999
Van Nuys, CA 91409
(818) 780-3951

National Coalition for the Prevention of Drug and Alcohol Abuse
537 Jones Road
Granville, OH 43023
(614) 587-2800

National Federation of Parents for Drug-Free Youth
8730 Georgia Avenue, Suite 200
Silver Spring, MD 20910
(30l) 585-5437

NCA
National Council on Alcoholism, Inc.
12 West 21st Street, 7th Floor
New York, NY 10010
(800) NCA-CALL

NCADI
National Clearinghouse for Alcohol/Drug Information
P. O. Box 2345
Rockville, MD 20852
(301) 468-2600

NIAAA
National Institute on Alcohol Abuse and Alcoholism
Room 16-105
Parklawn Building
5600 Fishers Lane
Rockville, MD 20857
(301) 443-3885

NIDA
National Institute on Drug Abuse
Room 10-05
Parklawn Building
5600 Fishers Lane
Rockville, MD 20857
(301) 443-6480

PRIDE
National Parents Resource Institute on Drug Education
Robert W. Woodruff
Volunteer Service Center, Suite 1002
100 Edgewood Avenue
Atlanta, GA 30303
(404) 651-2548

SADD
Students Against Drunk Driving
P. O. Box 800
277 Main Street
Marlboro, MA 01752
(800) 521-SADD

Note: Many more resources are available to teachers in most com-munities across the United States. For example, the following orga-nizations are involved in activities to prevent the early use of alcohol and other drugs: Girl Scouts of America, Inc., Girls' Clubs, Boys' Clubs, Lions' Clubs International, Kiwanis, 4-H, Freemasons, American Academy of Pediatrics, American Academy of Family Physicians, American Bar Association, and many others.

Appendix D: Training Manual

The following represents the basic contents of a support group leader training manual.

Mission Statement

Note: Create this statement by describing the conditions in your community and the values of your school or organization that underlie the program.

Glossary of Terms

Program Goals

1. to foster education and awareness among elementary children about chemicals and chemical dependence

2. to provide aid, support, and a place to process feelings in difficult times

Program Objectives

To help elementary (K-6) children:

1. learn about alcohol and other drugs

2. understand chemical dependence as a disease

3. learn how to identify and express feelings appropriately
4. learn problem-solving strategies and coping skills
5. develop a sense of community
6. overcome feelings of guilt, shame, and isolation
7. increase and celebrate self-awareness, self-esteem, and self-worth
8. have fun together

Program Description

The program will offer two distinctive types of support groups for elementary children:

- *Living Skills* groups
- *Concerned Persons* groups

Living Skills groups will be open to all children who seek to learn more about positive, healthy living skills. *Living Skills* groups will meet weekly for eight weeks.

Concerned Persons groups, for children who come from families with chemical dependence and its concurrent problems, will help members learn effective coping strategies. *Concerned Persons* groups will meet weekly for ten weeks.

Membership in both groups will be limited to six to ten children. Groups will be facilitated by trained leaders or co-leaders.

Training Requirements

To be considered for facilitator training, prospective group leaders must evidence the following qualities to some degree:

- love and empathy for children
- commitment and motivation
- interactive skills
- self-understanding and awareness
- some knowledge of chemical dependence or willingness to acquire it

Training Process

Prospective group leaders must take part in a three-phase training process:

1. Phase One—Observation and Orientation—involves leader trainees in a support group as observers and participants. This phase will last approximately 8 to 10 weeks (one full cycle of group sessions).

2. Phase Two—Apprenticeship—involves leader trainees in facilitating a support group along with a more experienced leader. This phase will last between 6 to 9 months and involve trainees in weekly group sessions. As in Phase One, trainees will be responsible for regular evaluation meetings with group leaders.

3. Phase Three—Co-leadership or Leadership—involves trainees in the actual and total facilitation of a support group, sharing equal responsibility for the activities and progress of the group with a more experienced leader. This training phase is ongoing.

Training Goals

Phase One Goals—To help trainees:

*   gain insight into their own child-like natures
*   proceed with any necessary healing
*   observe the procedures and strategies of small group facilitation in action

To attain Phase One goals, trainees must:

*   participate as a group member
*   be willing to disclose feelings
*   talk about what it was like in his or her family
*   share in all group activities and games
*   keep a log of observations and questions
*   take part in regular evaluation ("debriefing") meetings with the support group leader (trainer)

155

Phase Two Goals—To help trainees:

- share in the facilitation of a small group
- further personal growth and self-realization

To attain Phase Two goals, trainees must:

- assume responsibility and active leadership for at least one group activity per session
- continue to share in most group activities and games
- take part in regular evaluation ("debriefing") meetings with the support group leader (trainer)

Phase Three Goals—To help trainees:

- take responsibility for the leadership or co-leadership of a small group, a responsibility that includes:
  - planning group sessions
  - determining group activities
  - tracking group members' progress
  - identifying behavioral problems that may require individual therapy or other referrals
  - managing intra-group conflict
  - helping the withdrawn, quiet, or frightened child
- continue personal growth and self-realization
- assume responsibility for group evaluation
- share in program evaluation

To attain Phase Three goals, trainees must:

- work under the supervision of a more experienced preceptor
- take part in regular evaluation ("debriefing") meetings with the support group leader (trainer)
- take part in evaluative sessions with program staff

Supervision

During each phase of the training process, trainees will be supervised by a more experienced facilitator.

Community Resources

Note: In addition to the following national resources, include local, community referral agencies, self-help programs, and the school's counseling staff.

A. A.
Alcoholics Anonymous
General Service Office
P. O. Box 459
Grand Central Station
New York, NY 10163
(212) 686-1100

Al-Anon Family Group Headquarters
1372 Broadway
New York, NY 10018-0862
(212) 302-7240

Alateen
1372 Broadway
New York, NY 10018-0862
(212) 302-7240

Group leader candidates who take part in outside training sessions in addition to your in-house program can add to the manual any important materials they gained in their training.

Index

All italicized entries, unless otherwise indicated, are names of activities to be used in support groups.